The Language of Great

The Language of Great

Brenda Eagans

Trilogy Christian Publishers A Wholly Owned Subsidiary of Trinity Broadcasting Network
2442 Michelle Drive Tustin, CA 92780
Copyright © 2019 by Brenda Eagans
Scripture used by permission. Unless otherwise indicated all scripture is taken from the New King James Version®. Copyright © 1982 by Thomas Nelson. Used by permission. All rights reserved.
Scripture quotations marked (AMP) taken from the Amplified® Bible (AMP), Copyright © 2015 by The Lockman Foundation. Used by permission. www.Lockman.org
Scripture quotations marked MSG are taken from THE MESSAGE, copyright © 1993, 2002, 2018 by Eugene H. Peterson. Used by permission of NavPress. All rights reserved. Represented by Tyndale House Publishers, a Division of Tyndale House Ministries.
No part of this book may be reproduced, stored in a retrieval system or transmitted by any means without written permission from the author. All rights reserved. Printed in USA.
Rights Department, 2442 Michelle Drive, Tustin, CA 92780.
Trilogy Christian Publishing/ TBN and colophon are trademarks of Trinity Broadcasting Network.
For information about special discounts for bulk purchases, please contact Trilogy Christian Publishing.
Trilogy Disclaimer: The views and content expressed in this book are those of the author and may not necessarily reflect the views and doctrine of Trilogy Christian Publishing or the Trinity Broadcasting Network.
Manufactured in the United States of America
10 9 8 7 6 5 4 3 2 1
Library of Congress Cataloging-in-Publication Data is available.
ISBN: 978-1-64088-569-1
E-ISBN: 978-1-64088-570-7

Dedication

This book is dedicated to Prophet Ronnie Moore, an awesome man of God; my pastor and mentor of 14 years, at Word of Love Christian Center in Hurst, Texas. He has gone home to be with the Lord, his Savior, Jesus Christ. I pray God, You allow Pastor Ronnie to see this book and the impact his teaching and guidance had upon me, and still has on me, in my relationship with Jesus Christ! Thank you, Prophet Ronnie, for your love and heart in Christ!

Acknowledgements

I would like to thank Father God, His Son, Jesus Christ, and Holy Spirit for Their love and heart of revelation to make this book possible. I want to thank my sweet husband for his patience and his continued support in this endeavor. You pushed me to complete this book for my Savior, Jesus. Thank you, Windell, for your faith in our God—for knowing He gave me the talent and ability to write and finish this book for His glory!! Only in HIM am I…

Introduction

I watched a movie a few years ago and realized as I watched it, God was speaking to me about this very book. I have had this book in my spirit for years, since before I was born (that is what this book is all about; your future and the future of the Church). But the last ten years, God has revealed much to me about great faith. I have many messages about this topic. It is now time to reveal to others what God has revealed to me.

As I watched the movie, *Arrival*, I began to understand more about how my faith and God's future for me are dependent upon each other. Without going into all the details, the basic movie plot is this:

Twelve alien spaceships descend on earth in different countries. The aliens do not speak English, surprise! Countries around the world are trying to understand the language of the aliens, called Heptapods. In America a linguist, Louise Banks, is chosen to decipher the language of the aliens. The aliens use our word "weapon" in their language; therefore, humans believe the aliens are a threat to the world, because of the meaning of the word "weapon" in our language. But this word does not have the same meaning in the aliens' language. In truth, their language is a gift to the humans. The aliens do not understand time as a linear concept, but as more cylindrical.

Part of Louise's initial difficulty in translating the alien's language begins from her own "concept" of her language and view of time and reality. We write and speak sentences in a linear fashion (usually from left to right), where the images we depict are dependent on the way we order our words. The

Heptapods, however, rely on a form of signs and symbols as communication, telling the full story unbound by time, in one fell swoop. The Heptapods language is a form of circular symbols that never fully touch, perhaps implying the infinite possibilities of communication. At one point in the movie, the Russians are confused by the Heptapods who said, "There is no time." The Russians misunderstood this phrase to mean the aliens were saying, "Time is running out for the human," when it fact, the Heptapods meant the phrase literally; that their form of communication is independent from the human construct of time. The aliens communicate across the temporal sphere, and their language is unbound by the past, present, or future. Louise is challenged to see beyond the constraints of time as we see it.

Revealing the movie plot and the results of what happened in the movie is not my intention. My intention is for us as followers of Christ to open our eyes to see a different view of faith and time. The movie is not fact, it is a sci-fi film. That being said; let it open your senses to what could be possible in the spiritual realm. God is all-knowing. God is everywhere—all the time. Time was created by God and God resides outside of time. He is not dependent on a clock. God sees the end from the beginning. (See Isaiah 46:10.) God sees history and future as the same, they are not separate from one another—He sees it all at once. It is up to us, by faith, to walk in the unknown through His Holy Spirit. We have Christ in us, the power of the most Holy One in us, and all we have to do is ask and we will receive. It is time, as the Church, to ask for our eyes and ears to be opened to see and hear what the Spirit of the Lord is doing and saying in our lives!

Faith is not unfamiliar to any of us, we all have faith in

something or someone. Many have faith in man. Some have faith in their own abilities to get them where they desire to go. Some have faith in the nature of earth, that being the sun and moon. Some even have faith in Satan; I could go on and on. We have faith, that is confidence, that when we get into our car it will start. We have faith that as we sit in a chair it will hold us up. These are simple ways to view faith, but still, they are ways to show our faith in certain things.

In this book, I will be discussing the scriptures Jesus Himself speaks of when He says, "great faith" and the prophetic view of Who He is, what He has already accomplished in His view of time; and how we, by faith, can be in the place God has already prepared for us, before time began. This book is about His perfect will and plan for each of us and how we all interact with His divine purpose in His kingdom. Faith is the doorway we utilize to receive God's heavenly agenda. We have a future and a hope (see Jeremiah 29:11) in Christ and since we know this is true, by the Word of God, we know God desires His will for us. So how do we receive His best for us? All things will be revealed through His Holy Spirit. According to the Word of God, His Holy Spirit will teach us all things, revealing the heart of God to us. (See John 14:26.)

God has an agenda for His children, each individual's agenda works together and complements His agenda for the Body of Christ, His Church. God's plan can be likened to a tapestry of beautiful color—each thread filled with its own beauty and yet when it is added, intertwined with the other threads, each beautiful in their own—a picture develops, weaving the composite of them together, revealing the heart of the artist. In this case the Artist is our Creator God!

We are all part of a much bigger picture than just our own

individual world. God has a plan and a purpose for each one of us and our purpose is a part of His purpose for His glory! Everything is about God, His Son, Jesus Christ, Holy Spirit, and His glory. We are here because of His love for us—His heart for His creation. We are here in this realm to reflect His glory and walk in the Spirit realm, revealing God's glory on earth as it is in heaven! If we could just take our eyes off "self" and truly see through the eyes of God, remove the mirror of "self" and see the world as God does, it would amaze even the unbeliever. It is not by coincidence that God is releasing this book in a world of selfies, a world that is all about me and me and me. (I am sure there are many others in the world who God has revealed this concept to—I am not the only one God has shared this knowledge with.)

Are you ready to see things differently? See things through the eyes of the One Who created you? We must look at faith and time in a different view than ever before, we must look through the eyes of our Beloved One—the One Who died for each one of us, that we may live, and live more abundantly though Him! (See John 10:10.) I want everything God has prepared for me from before the foundations of the world and to receive this, I must seek Him, ask Him and receive from Him His perfect plan—not my own.

I know my purpose in the Kingdom of God and have learned to embrace what God has for me. My personal plan is a failure compared to the magnificent plan God has for my life. We must learn to discover His plan for us and then walk in it boldly, with His knowledge and courage. Fear will keep you from His plan, but faith will unravel the confusion and reveal His love for us! God's plans are good! We must come to the place of receiving only His best for us and letting go of our own selves, that is when heaven on earth will be revealed to us and we will walk in Him as never before. We will have success in all we do because we are in Him, fully embracing His will for us. If we would all let go and let God—the world would definitely be a different place.

As you read each chapter, stop and reflect on what Holy Spirit has revealed to you. Chew on the Word like a cow chews its cud; slowly and methodically regurgitating the contents until it is completely absorbed into your very being, naturally and spiritually as one.

Let us search the Scriptures and understand what God says about great faith, time, space, and the prophetic gift…

Chapter One

"Faith is at its truest and purest in this: We rest in 'what' God is."

Knowledge of the Holy, A.W. Tozer[1]

I read the above quote from A.W. Tozer's book, *Knowledge of the Holy*, and I would like to add to it. "Faith is at its truest and purest in this: We rest in what and Who God is."

As I have walked this journey with my Jesus, I rest in Who He is—not just what He is or what He does. God is love. (See 1 John 4:8, 16.) God is Spirit. (See John 4:24.) God is a consuming fire. (See Deuteronomy. 4:24 and Hebrews 12:29.) God is light. (See 1 John 1:5.) Who Christ is should not depend on my observation of Him, it should depend only on Him, God's written word of Him, and His character; not my interpretation. And yet, all too many times; Father God, Christ, and Holy Spirit are all thought of differently than Who They truly are based on "what" we have been taught about Them through man's eyes and reasoning. Isn't it time we see God through His own eyes?

The Word tells us to have faith in God. (See Mark 11:22.) We are to only trust in Him, for we know man can and will disappoint us, God knows this. That is why He tells us to trust Him—have faith in Him. If you do not know Who He is, how can you have faith in Him? So many times, we have been taught incorrectly by men's doctrine—some teach error intentionally for control or whatever purpose they choose. Many teach it unintentionally. They teach what they have learned,

---

[1] *Knowledge of the Holy, Tozer, A.W., page 62*

even though it may be in error. They do not seek God to find out if they are teaching His Word, according to His Word! No matter the reasons, false teaching has caused many to walk away from God, because they think God is something He is not. I pray as God reveals His heart in this book, you, the reader, will have a fresh understanding of Who God is and what He desires of you and for you. Let's look at faith and His Word! Hebrews 11:1-3 is one of the first Scriptures we will discuss as we release the understanding of the Word of God according to what God wants to say, not man.

> Now faith is the substance of things hoped for, the evidence of things not seen. For by it the elders obtained a good testimony. By faith we understand that the worlds were framed by the word of God, so that the things which are seen were not made of things which are visible.
>
> Hebrews 11:1-3

> Now faith is the assurance (title deed, confirmation) of things hoped for (divinely guaranteed), and the evidence of things not seen [the conviction of their reality—faith comprehends as fact what cannot be experienced by the physical senses]. For by this [kind of] faith the men of old gained [divine] approval. By faith [that is, with an inherent trust and enduring confidence in the power, wisdom and goodness of God] we understand that the worlds (universe, ages) were framed and created [formed, put in order, and equipped for their intended purpose] by the word of God, so that what is seen was

not made out of things which are visible.

Hebrews 11:1-3 (AMP)

"Faith is the substance…" The Greek word for substance is *hypostasis*—pronounced (*hü-po'-stä-sēs*). In this scripture the word "faith," means "*confidence, firm trust, assurance.*"[2] How many of us can say we are sure about the Word of God? Do we really believe Him? Not just believing in Him but believing Him! Are you confident in Who God is and what He has spoken over you, be it through His written Word, a rhema word, or a prophetic word? The answer to this question determines the measure of your faith! Do you firmly trust God and what He has said to you? Trust in Him and His Word! Many people talk (some too much) without saying anything worth hearing, and yet, we tend to trust man's word before we trust God's Word.

In this book, I am going to make some bold statements about faith, and I want us to understand that I can be bold based upon *my relationship* with my Father, His Son, Jesus, and His precious Holy Spirit. That is the key to our faith, our relationship with Father. We are certain to base our experience of fathers on the one we had growing up. For some it could be the absence of a father. Our own childhood relationships affect how we relate to others as we age. This perception skews our view of our Heavenly Father, because the only one we can compare Him to is the earthly dad we knew, or didn't know, as a child. So already, your perception of God is clouded by your previous encounters with men called "dad." In other words, we are unable to see Who God truly is, because when we hear the word "father," we have preconceived ideas of what that word

---

[2] *Blue Letter Bible; Strong's Concordance*

means, which affects our reaction to this word, "father."

I love my earthly father—I actually call him, "Daddy." He was a great dad to me growing up. Was he perfect? No, who is? No one is perfect. Was he always around? Maybe not, but it wasn't because he didn't want to be; it was because he had to work to support his family. Did I try him as a child? Of course I did, that was my personality. The one thing I can say about my earthly daddy is this: My daddy loves me. Did he always say the words "I love you?" No, and yet I knew my daddy loved me as a child. He still does, even more so now, even if he doesn't say it. Love is not about the words. Love is an action, not just a term we use for a feeling. I know my daddy loves me because he shows me daily. He took care of us as a family. He did what he had to so we were safe and secure.

When I was a horrible teen and young adult, my daddy never turned his back on me; that is real love. Many people tell me I am a different type of woman. Maybe that is true. I just know who I am, and I love me! Some need to hear the words, "I love you," often for the reassurance they are loved by a person. I know you love me by how you treat me. I do not need to hear "I love you," fifteen times a day. My sister, on the other hand, needed to hear the words, "I love you," for her to believe she was loved. We are different people needing different things from the men in our lives, based on who we are. Because of the different ways we received love, my sister and I each had a different perception of God, Who He is, and how He loves. My salvation experience was all I needed to know my heavenly Father loved me!

Before I knew Christ, I spent many years as a drug addict, and I wasn't a nice person. I wanted to be "right," but had difficulty getting there on my own. I did not think very highly of myself. That's where I was before I knew Christ. I was not a happy person, I was a junkie. Yes, I used needles and anything that would melt with water in a spoon to get high; my drug of choice was meth (speed). I will not go into detail about my past, but now you may understand where I was before I called on Jesus. I will, one day, release a book about my life and the testimony of God's pure love for me.

But for now, here is a quick glimpse of my past: One day in October of 1994, I called upon Jesus and He came and saved me and set me free, right where I was, in my bedroom. The same time I called upon Him to save me, He delivered me from drug addiction! Praise be to the Lord! I remember telling God, "I do not know You, but if You come and save me, help me, I will do whatever You ask me to do." Of course, there was more to the conversation than that, but you get the gist. I did not go to church as a child, so I really did not have any ideas about God—Who He was or what He was like. By faith, (faith in some Being called "God") I cried out and He heard me and answered my prayer! It was by faith in God, a God I knew nothing about; and by faith I reached out in desperation, knowing I needed Him, even though I did not know Him. I called on Him by faith and He answered me!

By faith I received salvation—that is, I believed in a God I could not see nor hear. I talked to this God I had never believed in before and He responded! By faith, one day so many years ago, I trusted in a God I did not know, and I believed I was going to go to heaven (a place I have never seen, only heard about). I was going to live forever! *What*??? We think we have little faith—ha! What faith it takes to receive salvation and believe God for Who and what He is! I am going to live eternally with my heavenly Father, His Son, Jesus, and Holy

Spirit. And by the way, this Jesus; He died a horrible death for me, in my place on a cross, and He was buried and then He rose from the grave three days later. Now that is faith! True faith is to call out to Father God and believe He is there and will respond! As we delve into the character of our heavenly Father and His concept of faith, let us look through the eyes of Father, through the lens of His world, and His heart!

Stop and seek Holy Spirit as you read through these pages. Rest, that is "selah" (pause) and listen to Him after a scripture or revelation stands out to you. Ask God what He wants reveal to you though His Word. Many times, to get though our daily assignments we read quickly—not this time. This book is about receiving and understanding God's truth; therefore pause, rest, pray, and "soak" after each chapter and receive Holy Spirit's revelation—it is just for you.

Chapter Two

In chapter one I began to bring a revelation of the Word of God in Hebrews 11. In this chapter I want to break down this Scripture, so we can truly understand what God is saying in His written word.

> Now faith is the substance of things hoped for, the evidence of things not seen. For by it the elders obtained a good testimony. By faith we understand that the worlds were framed by the word of God, so that the things which are seen were not made of things which are visible.
>
> Hebrews 11:1-3

> Now faith is the assurance (title deed, confirmation) of things hoped for (divinely guaranteed), and the evidence of things not seen [the conviction of their reality—faith comprehends as fact what cannot be experienced by the physical senses]. (2) For by this [kind of] faith the men of old gained [divine] approval. (3) By faith [that is, with an inherent trust and enduring confidence in the power, wisdom and goodness of God] we understand that the worlds (universe, ages) were framed and created [formed, put in order, and equipped for their intended purpose] by the word of God, so that what is seen was not made out of things which are visible.
>
> Hebrews 11:1-3 (AMP)

The word "faith" in Hebrews 11:1 is the Greek word "pistis." It is pronounced, pē'-stēs. This Greek word means, "the conviction of the truth, belief in God."[3] According to the Merriam-Webster Dictionary the word "faith" is defined as, "belief and trust in and loyalty to God; belief in the traditional doctrines of a religion; firm belief in something for which there is no proof." Faith, as we are discussing it in this book, is all about believing in God, even though you have not seen Him! Faith is about knowing God is real, believing He exists without seeing Him. If I see Him, then faith is not necessary. By faith we believe! Glory! I get excited just typing these words! Faith is confidence in our God—not in self—only in Him! Our confidence must be in God, in Christ, the Word manifested in the flesh, according to the book of John, through His Holy Spirit.

"And the Word became flesh and dwelt among us, and we beheld His glory, the glory as of the only begotten of the Father, full of grace and truth," John 1:14. Faith in God, Who He is, and what He has spoken (Christ) and the power (Holy Spirit) He has given to us.

Faith is the substance, the material of your hope. The Greek word for "substance" is "*hypostasis,*" pronounced *hü-po'-stä-sēs*. In this scripture the word "substance," means "standing under, support." The word "*hypostasis*" is a combination of two words: *Hupo*, "under," *histemi*, "to stand."[4] In Hebrews 11:1 it breaks down as this: "that which stands, or is set, under, a foundation, beginning; hence, the quality of confidence which leads one to stand under, endure, or undertake anything." And according to *Vines Complete Expository Dictionary*, it may signify "a title-deed, as giving a guarantee, or reality." When you look up

---

3   *Blue Letter Bible, Strong's Concordance*
4   *Blue Letter Bible, Strong's Concordance*

"substance" in the *Merriam-Webster's Dictionary* it is defined as, "essential nature or essence; a fundamental or characteristic part or quality and the ultimate reality that underlies all outward manifestations and change."

The word "substance" is the essence of faith, it is the title deed of ownership! Faith, that is your confidence, is the substance or the deed, the ultimate reality that supports all outward manifestations and change! When I think of substance, I think of something with weight. You can "feel" the substance, the essence of a thing. We are not finished revealing all God has said in this scripture, we have only just begun and already it is time to shout and praise the Lord for His goodness!

"Now faith is the substance of things hoped for, the evidence of things not seen." The next word to discuss in this scripture is "things." Things hoped for! "Things," in the Greek, is "*pragma*," pronounced *prä'g-mä*.[5] This word means, "that which is or exists, a thing." This word is just what it is, "a thing or things." Something that exists...where? In the spiritual and in the natural! Just because you do not see it in the natural, does not mean it does not exist. There is still a spiritual world beyond our natural eyes and just because you do not see it, does not mean it does not exist.

The word "hope" tells us this; "to expect or trust." The Greek word is "*elpizō*," pronounced *el-pē'-zō*.[6] In *Webster's Dictionary* the word "hope" means this: "to cherish a desire with anticipation; to want something to happen or be true; to desire with expectation of obtainment or fulfillment; and to expect with confidence." Things hoped for—things expected—things trusted in Christ. Paul is talking about the people who went

---

5   *Blue Letter Bible, Strong's Concordance*
6   *Blue Letter Bible, Strong's Concordance*

before himself and others (including us) and their faith in God and His promises—All He promised!

"The evidence of things not seen." The "evidence." Who thought evidence has anything to do with faith? This part of the sentence almost seems to contradict what the apostle is trying to relay about faith. In the Greek language, the word "evidence" is "*elegchos*," pronounced *e'-len-khos*.[7] In the Greek this word means, "a proof, that by which a thing is proved or tested; that by which invisible things are proved and we are convinced of their reality." When I think of the word "evidence" I usually associate it with police work or science, or a way to prove what I already suspected. Faith is actually the evidence of those things we do not see. What things? All things visible and invisible, according to Colossians 1:15-17. (We will cover this Scripture in the next chapter). Faith produces the invisible in the visible realm! Let's read Hebrews 11:1 again as it is in the Greek language—defined and raw.

Now faith (the firm belief in God and all He is) is the substance (the material, the realization, that which stands, or is set, under, a foundation, beginning) of things (that which is or exists) hoped (to expect; trust) for, the evidence (proof) of things not seen (not seen with the physical eye; not manifested, yet).

Now the firm belief in God is the realization of that which exists, to trust the proof of things not seen yet by the physical eye. Faith comprehends as fact what cannot be experienced by the physical senses. Stop for a minute and take this scripture into your spirit. We try, continuously, to reason with our minds what God is revealing—Stop! Rest! Breathe in Holy Spirit and ask Him to reveal what He just spoke, as you release your mind and depend on the Spirit of God to speak to you. It

---

7   *Blue Letter Bible, Strong's Concordance*

is time for the Body of Christ to open her eyes to see past the black type on the white pages and ask, seek revelation of HIM! That is what faith is all about; it is believing He is and walking with Him in His heavenly realm to bring Him (His revelation) into this earthly realm. Why? For change! To change what? To change this earth to reflect Him once again as it did in the beginning! To fellowship with Him and release His presence on earth! What a difference a little faith can make.

Faith is my belief in God. Faith is the material, my realization of things that do not exist in this present realm manifesting themselves on earth as they are in heaven. Remember, we are observing His word in the realm of faith, the prophetic realm of His Holy Spirit. As we continue our study (that is really what this book is) of His written word about faith opening up a new understanding for those who are walking in defeat and disappointment in their lives, do not limit God or yourself in Him! Receive His promises by faith!

Chapter Three

As we noted in the previous chapter faith births, or brings forth, what we cannot see into the realm of what we can see. That is one of the simplest definitions of faith I can release. In this chapter, we will continue to reveal the Scriptures through breaking down the meanings of words and phrases in the Bible. Please stay with me as we discover what God is saying so we can correctly apply it in our lives.

Birthing is uncomfortable, as well as painful, and yet it is always worth the time and struggle when you see the results of your labor. The Word of God is no different; you will see the fruit of your labor as you press in and receive what God revels to the Church. I mentioned Colossians 1:15-17 in chapter two. Now it is time to release God's knowledge regarding this Scripture.

> He (Jesus) is the image of the invisible God, the firstborn over all creation. For by Him all things were created that are in heaven and that are on earth, visible and invisible, whether thrones, or dominions or principalities or powers. All things were created through Him and for Him. And He is before all things, and in Him all things consist.
> Colossians 1:15-17

I love to study the Word of God and for the years I have known my Savior, I haven't studied enough. There is always more and more to know of God, Christ, and His Holy Spirit. I do have my favorite books in the Bible; the Book of John is my favorite gospel. Ephesians and Colossians are probably my two favorite epistles in the New Testament. And yes, I have many favorites in the Old Testament, too. I believe you cannot study enough, pray enough, or receive enough revelation before you go home to be with Him, eternally.

"He is the IMAGE of the invisible God, the firstborn over all creation" (Colossians 1:15).

"Jesus said to him, 'Have I been with you so long, and yet you have not known Me, Philip? He who has seen Me has seen the Father; so how can you say, 'Show us the Father?'" (John 14:9)

Jesus is the image of God. This word "image" in the Greek language is "*eikon*," it is pronounced (ā-kō'n). This word means, "figure, likeness, a likeness (literally) a statue, profile, or (figuratively) representation or resemblance."[8] According to *Vine's Expository* the word "image" denotes, "an image," the word involves two ideas of representation and manifestation. Jesus Christ is the likeness of God. Jesus and God are One.

"That they all may be one, as You, Father are in Me, and I in You; that they may also be one in Us, that the world may believe that You sent Me" (John 17:21).

Jesus is not just a reflection of God, He is God! He only does what He sees the Father do. Jesus only says what He hears the Father speak. In the *Merriam-Webster Dictionary* "image" is defined as: "the external (visual) representation of a person or thing." Jesus represents God, not just in His physical form. When we speak of "image," it is not only "who or what we see." "Image" also describes who the person represents, the character of the one seen. This may be difficult for some of us to comprehend, because we know God as an invisible Be-

---

8   *Blue Letter Bible, Strong's Concordance*

ing; One we cannot touch or see—not so. "Image" denotes the character of the One represented. The image of God in Christ represents His love for all humanity; represents His grace and mercy, His peace and compassion. So, an image is not only the visible form of the representative; it is also the spiritual form; that is, the character, impression, essence of the One the Image represents! Jesus is the heart of God represented to the world.

Invisible. Jesus is the form of the invisible God. The Greek word for the term, "invisible" is "*aoratos*," pronounced ä-o'-rä-tos. This word is defined as "unseen." The definition does not say it is a thing that does not exist, it says it cannot be seen. Think about this for just a moment: "Invisible" means, "you cannot see it." You may ask yourself, "Isn't that the same thing as it does not exist?" No! Just because you cannot see something does not mean it does not exist. You cannot see the wind, but it exists, and you know this because you see and feel the effects of the wind. You feel the wind on your face, and you can see the leaves moving on a tree because of the wind.

"For since the creation of the world His invisible attributes are clearly seen, being understood by the things that are made, even His eternal power and Godhead, so that they are without excuse" (Romans 1:20).

God may be invisible to you, and yet you can still see His effect on His creation! Children can be so very honest. Have you ever wondered how they know "Someone" made the world? When a child asks about the world, they do not ask "how" the world was made, they ask, "Who made the trees, or the mountains, or the sea? Who made all this?" God may be invisible, and yet, even a child knows He exists.

There is a spiritual realm that we can bring into this earthly realm by faith. The heavens are already open—the veil was torn from top to bottom when Christ died on the cross, opening the holy of holies to us. We now have access to God and all He encompasses without hesitation. When God speaks of the natural and the spiritual, is there really any difference for Him? The invisible is visible before God, just as the visible (this realm) is before Him. Jesus has created all things—things you can see and things you cannot see. They all exist in Him.

"For by Him all things were created that are in heaven and that are on earth, visible and invisible, whether thrones, or dominions or principalities or powers. All things were created through Him and for Him" (Colossians 1:16).

God speaks of the spiritual realm as His reality. And by faith it becomes our reality! Stop a minute and receive this word—all things—visible and invisible are made in Him and by Him.

"Now the Lord is the Spirit; and where the Spirit of the Lord is, there is liberty" (2 Corinthians 3:17).

This Scripture is one that often is quoted, referring to our freedom from the enemy or self. And yet, when you read the context surrounding this verse you find a very different understanding. Paul is speaking of the veil being removed and the glory of God transforming us into His image. Where God is there is freedom; freedom to understand the truth of Who He is and what He has done through Jesus' shed blood on the cross, His resurrection and His ascension, sitting at the right hand of the Father, in the heavenly places. The veil was placed over the heavens after the fall of man, Adam and Eve. Prior to their sin, Adam and Eve had full access to God and all He is. The veil cut off our access to heaven, where God abides. We closed the door, the access to God, through our disobedience. Now through the shed blood of Christ, we are free to know and understand the heavenly realm.

Through Christ, the veil has been torn from the top to the bottom and now the heavens are once again open to God's children. (See Matthew 27:51; Mark 15:38; Luke 23:45.) What does that mean for us? It means we have full access, again, to God through Christ! In Him, Christ, all things were made. He was in the beginning with God and is God. (See John 1:1-5.)

"All who dwell on the earth will worship him, whose names have not been written in the Book of Life of the Lamb slain from the foundation of the world" (Revelation 13:8.)

Jesus has always been and will always be. Jesus was before the created world and all things were created in Him and through Him. What things? All things; things seen, and things not seen. My question to you today is, do you believe that God created all things in His Son? Do you believe through the cross you have access to all these things? Access to the things of God, the understanding and knowledge of a different reality, His reality?

I desire Him over everything else in this world. When I seek Him for these unseen things I search for the spiritual things of God, His knowledge to be shared, His wisdom released to me in unknown realities.

> "That the God of our Lord Jesus Christ, the Father of glory, may give to you the spirit of wisdom and revelation in the knowledge of Him, the eyes of your understanding being enlightened; that you may know what is the hope of His calling, what are the riches of the glory of His inheritance in the saints.
>
> Ephesians 1:17-18

I can ask for things in this world, material things. The things of this world are temporal and hold no solid meaning, except to glisten in the eyes of man. I desire my eyes be opened to the spiritual things of God, so I may make an impact in the natural world He created for me. We often don't realize, or maybe we just forget, as sons and daughters of God we will live on this earth again. Heaven will come down and abide in this realm once Christ returns. Read Revelation 21. Powerful! These are the things I desire! The understanding and revelation of HIM. I just want to know Him, intimately.

In the Scripture, Paul says by Christ, "…all things were created, that are in heaven and that are on earth, visible and invisible, whether thrones, or dominions or principalities or powers. All things were created through Him and for Him" Colossians 1:16.

Looking deeper into the heart of this message, let's reveal what Paul is trying to convey to us, that we may understand His holy word for us. The word "created" here is the Greek word *ktizō*, pronounced *ktē'-zō*. According to the *Blue Letter Bible* this word means, "to create—of God creating the worlds—to form, shape, i.e. to completely change or transform (through the idea of proprietorship of the manufacturer); to fabricate, i.e. found (form originally)."

How did God create? According to Genesis 1, He spoke. God spoke and there was light. God spoke and there was land. God spoke and the atmosphere was created. God spoke and the animals of the earth and the seas were created. God spoke, creating all things. We have the power to create as well. When I say create, I am saying, "bring the invisible things from the spiritual world into the natural world." God is the Creator of all things. He has given us the ability to bring these things into the world through our faith in Him.

God created, that is "formed," all things in heaven and on earth. We know and understand the term "earth," that is the natural place we abide. Heaven is the abode of God. Heaven is the region where God dwells, with the heavenly angels. According to the Greek terminology the word "heaven" used in Colossians 1:16 is *ouranos*, pronounced ü-rä-nos. This word means, "The vaulted expanse of the sky with all things visible in it; the universe, the world ; the aerial heavens or sky, the region where the clouds and the tempests gather, and where thunder and lightning are produced; the sidereal or starry heavens ; the region above the sidereal heavens, the seat of order of things eternal and consummately perfect where God dwells and other heavenly beings. This word is from a root meaning 'to cover' or 'encompass.'"[9]

In heaven, the word of God is settled. In other words, God's word is, "establish, to be fixed." (See Psalm 119:89.) Just like at your home, your word is the "law" so to speak; your household knows the word you have established as rules and expectations. The same goes for God—in heaven no one questions God's word as truth and the standard. His word goes forth without any hindrances and so should our word go forth here on earth in His Name and power by faith!

The word "visible," of course, is defined as, "open, being able to see, gaze at." The word "invisible" would be just the opposite. It means it is something you cannot see. This does not mean the invisible things do not exist, it just means that we, at this time, cannot see them. These things have not become visible, yet. By faith, the invisible can and will become visible to you as you walk in Christ and understand His heart for you!

---

[9] *Strong's Concordance*

We know what the visible things are because we can see them. We can see what we want or need. The home, or car, or job or whatever "it" is. The spiritual, or the invisible things, are not so easily discerned. When Paul speaks of the invisible, he speaks of the authority of the spirit realm. He talks about the thrones, dominions, principalities and powers of the spirit realm. This where our true identity is in Christ, in the spiritual places. By faith we are to bring the spiritual into the natural.

The word "thrones" in the Greek is *thronos*, and it is defined as, "a throne, a seat of authority." *Vine's Expository* states it is, "by metonymy for angelic powers of one who holds dominion or exercises authority; thus, in plural of angels, a stately seat ("throne"); by implication, power or (concretely) a potentate." We hold a place on these thrones, too. Unfortunately, most Christians are unaware of where God has seated them in Christ. We must remember we have inherited the kingdom of God through Christ. When you inherit something, it is yours and all that it entails is yours, too. You have inherited a seat at the table with God—sit down and partake of your new life.

In America, we have difficulty understanding thrones and kingdoms because we live in a Republic. We do not have a king nor queen, nor a dictator residing over us as a people. Christ has been given ALL authority over ALL kingdoms of this world and in the age to come. In kingdoms, the King speaks and whatever He says is carried out immediately. Study kingdoms and how they are set up, then take that knowledge and apply it to God and His kingdom. I believe it will be an eye-opener for you as this knowledge and understanding is released.

The word "dominions" is *kyriotēs*, pronounced *kü-rē-o'-tās*, meaning, "power, lordship, mastery, rulers." This also applies to kingdom rule and the unseen forces that play havoc on this world. There are many fallen angels who pretend to hold authority, using their power to release the enemy's plan for a territory instead of God's perfect will for that part of the world. Why this happens seems to perplex man, "Why does God let these things continue?" Maybe it's because the church, His bride, His body, is not walking in her set place. What good is it to have authority and power yet never use it?

From the beginning, God gave us this earth and the authority to watch over it. The problem is, most of God's people do not know this truth or if they do, they choose not to walk in their God-given right!

"Then God blessed them, and God said to them, 'Be fruitful and multiply; fill the earth and subdue it; have dominion over the fish of the sea, over the birds of the air, and over every living thing that moves on the earth'" (Genesis 1:28.)

The word "principalities" is the Greek word *archē*, pronounced är-kh. This word is describing the "'first place,' principality, rule, magistracy of angels and demons." It can also denote "the beginning, origin; that is the person or thing that commences, the first person or thing in a series, the leader." Paul uses this word to describe the angels and demons holding dominions, placed in that position in the created order of things.

This is the truth; the enemy should not have any power over any place a child of God resides! We were the first to have the dominion over the earth. It was given to us by God. He created the earth and He can give the earth to whomever He pleases. He gave it to us, humanity; Adam and Eve. We, in turn, gave dominion of the earth to Satan. Now through the blood Christ and His death on the cross we have been given back what we gave away! You and I have authority, by faith, to walk in victory over every serpent and scorpion. This why the next word in Colossians 1:16 is so important to comprehend.

The word "powers," which is the Greek word *exousia*, pronounced *eks-ü-sē'-a*[10]. More than any other definition, this word denotes "authority." It can also describe "privilege or delegated influence." When used in Colossians 1:16 it means: "the leading and more powerful among created beings superior to man, spiritual potentates; used in the plural of a certain class of angels." The other Greek word used for "power" is *dunamis*, where we get our English word, "dynamite." This word is related to "energy"—the "power of the punch" (so to speak). *Exousia* in contrast, means the "authority" to use the *dunamis*, that is, the "power to punch." The enemy has power (*dunamis*), we know that, but since the cross, he has no authority (*exousia*) to wield that power. He lost the authority to use his power! Glory to God!

In Luke 10:17-20, the Scripture is clear that Satan has fallen from heaven, losing his authority, and now you have the authority on this earth over all his power! Yes, we have power, the enemy has power. The difference between us and Satan is this, we have the authority to use our power and shake up the spiritual realm and the earthly realm! The enemy has lost his authority! We have gained authority in Christ!

The thrones, dominions, principalities, and powers of the invisible world exist and their affect is seen in this visible world. When you study this Scripture, as well as Ephesians 6 on the warfare of the Believer, you understand that Jesus made all the visible and the invisible and He has authority over them all. He is seated in the heavenly realm above all the powers of this realm. He sits at the right hand of God. Do you believe

---

[10] *Strong's Concordance*

you have the authority to speak the invisible into the visible by faith in God?

The issue with most of us is this: We do not know what Jesus has given to us and how to receive what He has for us. When we search the Scriptures, we find Jesus and all He has given to us through the cross. But what is simple, men have complicated. What is it you need from God right now? Is it something in this natural realm? Is it a job? Does your marriage need restoration? Do you need a new car? Maybe you are looking for a deeper relationship with God. Maybe you desire gifts from Father—spiritual gifts. Maybe you need peace and rest. How many of us consistently walk in this in Christ? The spiritual things will manifest into this earthly realm, once you receive them by faith. In other words, whether they are things in the natural or of the spirit, God has already created the things you desire from Him and they exist in your world by faith. Whatever you need or want—you can find it in Christ.

This is not a "name-it-and-claim-it" faith theology. This is not a new age way to get things for yourself. What I am speaking of is understanding Who God is and What He has done, through His Son, Jesus Christ! Believing not only in Him but believing Him; that is, believe what He says and what He shares as Truth.

Many years ago as a new creation in Christ, I went to an awesome, spirit-filled church and God allowed a beautiful woman, one of His daughters, to reach out to me and help me understand this new place I had entered as a believer. She and I studied the word, and she taught me to study "who" I was, by studying "Who" Christ is. One of the many ways she ministered to me was through a study of the Word of God, where I was to read through the New Testament and write down every

Scripture that said, "in Christ," "in Him," "in Jesus," "through Christ," "through Him," "through Jesus," etc. I wrote down and took in to my spirit all I am in Him. I still have these scriptures and in fact, I have done this numerous times in my walk. It strengthened me to know Who Christ is, and who I am in Him! We must not forget who we are in Christ. We have authority because we are in a kingdom—the Kingdom of God. We represent Him before the world, meaning we are to be Who He is in this world. Do you know, truly know, who you are in Christ?

Let's finish this study so we can move on to the "meat" of this book!

"And He is before all things, and in Him all things consist" (Colossians 1:17.)

Christ has always been and will always be. He was before all things. All things consist in Him.

The word "consist" is the Greek word *synistēmi*, pronounced *sün-ē'-stä-mē*; meaning, "to place together, to set in the same place, to bring or band together; to comprehend, to put together by way of composition or combination, to teach by combining and comparing, establish, exhibit, to put together, unite parts into one whole; to be composed of, consist; to set together."[11]

In the *Vine's Expository Dictionary* it is described as this: "sun, 'with,' histemi, 'to stand,' denotes, in its intransitive sense, 'to stand with or fall together, to be constituted, to be compact.'" It is said of the universe as upheld by the Lord, Colossians 1:17, "by Him all things stand together."

There is not one thing created that was not created in Christ and by Christ. He "holds together" all things. Without

---

11 Strong's Concordance

Christ, everything would fall apart! He made it all. (See John 1.) Remember, Jesus is the Word of God spoken into existence. He is the image of God in all His glory!

Take time to pray and meditate upon the things God has revealed to you in this chapter. You may already know and understand these truths. Either way—stop and relax, rest in Him, and ask Holy Spirit to open your eyes to see and your ears to hear what He would say to you in this spiritual knowledge of faith in Him.

Chapter Four

I pray I have set a foundation in the first few chapters; an understanding of God and our faith in Him. There is still so much more to discuss, and even by the time we finish the book and close the last chapter, there will be more to study and to release. That is the way the word of God works, the more you study and understand, the more He reveals to you. Ask, seek, and knock, it will be opened.

When we can receive and understand the process of the previous chapters, our entire mindset is changed. We no longer look at this world as the only possibility—we are able to look "past" into the spiritual realm, where all things exist! It is time the Body of Christ thinks like Christ thinks. To think with a renewed mind, as Romans 12:2 says, "we are not conformed to this world, but we are transformed by the renewing of our mind," we must "see'" things differently.

The last chapter's intent was to open our eyes to see and know what He sees. Will we fully understand before we go home to be with Him? More than likely, no. And yet, there are some who saw more than others; a man who walked with Him and knew Him, understanding His ways on this earth until he walked right into heaven with Him Yes, I am speaking of Enoch.

Adam was still alive when Enoch was living. Did they know each other? Did Adam tell Enoch of the garden and his intimate time with God? Do you believe the stories of God, as Adam first knew Him, were told through-out the tribes, handed down like folklore? Is it possible that Enoch had heard these stories since he was a young boy, and he longed for that relationship with God? I do not know any of this for sure, but I do ask God and seek His wisdom in the history of my ancestors, because Holy Spirit knows all things, He will share with me what I do not know in His own timing.

Enoch walked with God for three-hundred years before he "was no more" on earth. (See Genesis 5:21-24.) Enoch probably experienced more of God than any other man on earth, excluding Christ. Enoch learned how to walk with God, not only in this earthly realm, but also in the spiritual realm. The Scripture states, "Enoch walked with God three hundred years… Enoch walked with God; and he was not, for God took him" (Genesis 5:22, 24).

Do you believe it is possible Enoch had seen heaven before God took him home for the last time? I do! I believe Enoch walked in this realm and the heavenly realm of God while he was still on this earth. Remember, Enoch walked with God. He walked where God walked. God did not walk with Enoch. Enoch walked so close with God that one day, God just brought him up to heaven, bypassing physical death. He walked into his glorious body.

When I teach in certain places, some say to me, "But Prophetess, he did not have a glorious body at that time, for Christ had not come and died on the cross and rose again." I would say to you, get out of the religious mindset of this realm and natural time only. There is more to life than what you see, and you have access to it! Scripture says Christ was with God in the beginning and He was slain before the foundation of the world. (See Revelation 13:8.)

In the mind of God, everything was complete before the world was ever formed. The possibilities in Christ are endless.

Get out of the old and get into the new wineskin! Stop looking at what you can see with your physical eyes and move into the realm of God's mind and the possibilities in Him! Take hold of the mind of Christ and look through your spiritual eyes at a world created just for us!

Enoch did not let this world hold him back from being with God, he knew God like no other in his day! His faith went beyond—went beyond this world into the world of God; that is, heaven and all of which it consists! It is possible to easily move from this realm to heaven in Christ. Only God and Enoch know exactly what went on between them. To seek God for answers is a continual walk!

"Enoch" in Hebrew is the word *Chanowk*, it is pronounced *khan·ōke'*. This word means, "dedicated or initiated" in Hebrew. The root for this word means, "(properly), to narrow; (figuratively), to initiate or discipline:—dedicate, train up."[12] Enoch walked with God.

"Can two walk together, unless they are agreed?" (Amos 3:3).

When we walk with God, we are saying to Him, "We agree with You, Your Word, and Holy Spirit." Enoch dedicated himself to God, he lived out his name. Enoch initiated a different relationship with God than most in his time. He initiated a "new way'" as he dedicated himself to God, not just to God's ways, but he dedicated himself to Who God truly was! Enoch was interested in God Himself! The desire Enoch had for God was not based on what God could give him, it was based on Who God is—His heart—that is love! Many of us seek God only for His promises, it is time we seek Him for Him! I believe Enoch sought a true relationship with his God, our

---

12   Strong's Concordance

God. Enoch walked in this world and the spiritual realm for three-hundred years! Enoch started a new thing, a new way to relate to God the Father!

The root meaning of the name of "Enoch" is "to narrow or train up," as we discussed earlier. God was opening the door to a new (narrow) way to Him; a preview, so to speak, of His plan in the New Testament. Not everyone will find the way. Not everyone will see the way. The narrow way is a way we must find as we look deeper into Christ. The Body of Christ (I am included) tends to look for what God can do for us rather than just seeking Him and His heart. Enoch sought God, for He is, fully.

"Enter by the narrow gate; for wide is the gate and broad is the way that leads to destruction, and there are many who go in by it. Because narrow is the gate and difficult is the way which leads to life, and there are few who find it" (Matthew 7:13-14).

What did Enoch see? What did he experience? I believe Enoch walked in this earth and with God in the heavenlies, because that was God's desire, to be with this man who wanted to be with Him! Enoch surpassed the concept of time as we know it. He did not let time hinder him in this realm, he actually walked in and out of time with God. God is not hindered by time, so when we are with Him, we are out of time, as we understand it. We will live in eternity with God, that is His reality. There is no time in heaven, except what God chooses to reveal as time.

"When He opened the seventh seal, there was silence in heaven for about half an hour" (Revelation 8:1).

God chose to share with John the amount of time that had passed. He did not have to, and yet, for some reason, God chose to share this information. Some have said, "Well how can there be time in heaven if there is not time in God?" God revealed the amount of time that had passed according to human senses for the purpose of our understanding. God can do anything He chooses to do, any way He chooses to do it, based on His character and Word. We must stop looking at Him with limitations and look at our Heavenly Father as the Possibility!

"All things are possible to him who believes" (Mark 9:23).

When I am in prayer and "lost" in Him, time is irrelevant and non-existent. I will be in prayer, or worship, or in a vision with Him and time cannot be measured by my human intellect. I remember a time in worship and prayer when I was on my face before God. During this time, as I was bowed down upon the floor, the Lord Himself came into the room. I could see the train of His robe as He walked past me. I could not lift my face up to look at Him, as His glory overwhelmed me to the place where like Isaiah said, " …for I am undone." I could not raise my head to look into the face of my holy God, for I was shaking and trembling in reverence of His holy Presence. The train of His robe glistened the brightest white I have never seen on this earth. I was taken to a place in the spirit where His Presence, His Glory totally took over my entire being! I felt as though time was standing still. He continued to walk by, what seemed like forever, as I was frozen in this sweet moment of revelation. Time and space were irrelevant to me at that moment; all I wanted to do was remain on the ground and worship Him as He passed by me. I cannot tell you how long I was on the floor or how much time passed; the experience was too glorious, nothing mattered but HIM.

In Christ, "all things are possible," (Matthew 19:26; Mark

9:23; Mark 10:27; Mark 14:36). God has opened the realm of His heaven to us through the death, burial, resurrection, and ascension of His Son, Jesus Christ! God can do what He wants, when He wants. His only boundary is His own Word! He will do all things through what He has spoken. Think about this Scripture, "…if indeed you continue in the faith, grounded and steadfast, and are not moved away from the hope of the gospel which you heard, which I preached to every creature under heaven, of which I, Paul, became a minister" (Colossians 1:23).

Paul says the gospel has already been preached to every creature under heaven. It is already done, we are here to fulfill what God has already ordained. In HIM it is done! Walk in Him, walk with Him, walk through Him!

I am not writing this book to argue theology or other intentions or beliefs about the Scriptures. What God has revealed to me, I reveal to the Body of Christ. I am writing this book to give His people (all people) the opportunity to see past the white pages with black type and see the length, the depth, the width, and the height of His love.(See Ephesians 3:18.) Look into the eyes of your Beloved One and receive ALL He is! Think about this for just a moment. Ask Holy Spirit to release holy revelation to you about God, Christ, and Holy Spirit—the visible and the invisible. See the invisible right before your eyes.

Chapter Five

How do you get there? How do you believe and know who you are in Christ? You must go deeper into Who Christ is. Consider what has He done and how to access all He has given you through His death, burial, resurrection, and ascension? He is seated at the right hand of the Father, according to Hebrews 8:1, His Father—our Father. I am in Him and He is in me, we are One. (See John 14:20.)

When you look into the Face of God, the Love of Christ, the Person of Holy Spirit, you find yourself lost in Who They are. In John 17, Jesus consistently prays for us to be one with Him and His Father. He only glorifies His Father. We are to glorify only Him. That is what you do when you are one—you do for the other first. Your heart is always before the One. My Father desires to be One with me, His creation. Why? To share His glory? No, to give back His glory in the works I do in His Son, Jesus Christ.

According to many scriptures, Jesus Christ had the option to do His own will. When He was in the garden His prayer was this, "He went a little farther and fell on His face, and prayed, saying, 'O My Father, if it is possible, let this cup pass from Me; nevertheless, not as I will, but as You will'" (Matthew 26:39).

"Or do you think that I cannot now pray to My Father, and He will provide Me with more than twelve legions of angels?" (Matthew 26:53).

Jesus made a choice to do the Fathers' will, not His own. Christ questioned His Father, even though He knew the answer. He did not want to die on the cross, and yet, He died for me and you. It was the only way. He chose to lay His life down for us.

"My soul is exceedingly sorrowful even unto death..." (Matthew 26:38).

"I am the living bread which came down from heaven. If anyone eats of this bread, he will live forever; and the bread that I shall give is My flesh, which I shall give for the life of the world" (John 6:51).

The Father's desires became Jesus' desires, even to the point of death. I hear many brothers and sisters quote Revelation 12:11, but only partially—this is what I hear, "And they overcame him by the blood of the Lamb and the word of their testimony." But the full version of this Scripture is: "And they overcame him by the blood of the Lamb, and the word of their testimony, and they did not love their lives to the death."

Many believers just quote the first part of Revelation 12:11, about the blood of the Lamb and the word of their testimony, however, it is the last part that truly means you have become one with Christ. If you can lay your life down for Him, for His sake, then you have truly given up everything in this world! Your eyes are on Him and Him alone.

When we are One with Him, our desires become His desires...not our own. Your heart becomes His heart for this world, and beyond. You see hurting people and you want to do something, anything for people in lack, in lack in the spirit realm. You do not know how to help relieve the pain of the broken, but Holy Spirit knows. People need more than a prayer and move on; they need the signs, miracles, and wonders of the spirit world. How do we bring that heaven to this world?

You are ONE with Christ. The same resurrection power that raised Him from the dead abides in you, lives in you, dwells in you. This power fills the very essence of who you are. Not only do you carry this supernatural power in you, you also carry the authority to use that power for the good of this earthly realm, removing the powers and principalities that currently reign over this earth. We are a force to be reckoned with in this world. Unfortunately, the Church does not know who she is in Christ. Those who are aware change the atmosphere around them by removing the ungodly and releasing the godly; that is, Holy Spirit power in any given place they abide.

Before I get into the chapters about "great faith," the Lord wants us to understand the power and authority we carry. Faith is not just asking for things in this realm. Faith is about bringing the "invisible" into the visible realm. Please hear my heart. Yes cars, houses, things here on earth are necessary, and you can receive many of these things by faith and the principles of God's kingdom. (And other ways, too, like hard work.) I am here to discuss the power and authority coming into this realm to change the lives of those without Him! Those sick, lame, hurting, oppressed, depressed, dying in a hurting world.

Your faith looks past today and breaks the barrier between heaven and earth; the veil is already removed, the only thing holding heaven from fully releasing His glory is our faith. Ouch! My position as a prophetess in this realm is to release the words God has given in a "kairos" time, an opportune time, the time the word births. God releases me to go into territories to take the land back for His glory. Too long we have used our faith to fill our own pockets, how about fulfilling God's will in His season? As I see heaven come down into the earthly realm, I am constantly amazed at how God moves and prepares the time for a new thing to emerge from heaven.

His word is settled in heaven. No one or no thing can stop the word of God in heaven. Why should it be different in this realm? The places where unbelief and doubt filled the atmosphere were the places where Jesus was unable to perform miracles. It is not uncommon in the gospels to see Jesus bring only a few close friends (John, James and Peter) with Him during times when it was important for faith to be at its strongest. Please note, there were many times the disciples' faith was not where it should be, but God is faithful, even when we are not. I remind people in many messages I preach, do not say, "I don't know," when you get in a situation where you do not know what to do; instead, ask Holy Spirit to help you. He already has the answer you need. Just ask and He will release the answer to you, in His time! Holy Spirit glorifies Christ and Christ glorifies the Father. You and I are one with Them, so ask when you pray, and you will receive! (See Mark 11:24.). Your prayer is communication with God. Just talk with Him and He will respond.

Many times, we, brothers and sisters in Christ, think prayer is this "thing" that is so spiritual, it cannot be articulated. Prayer is a conversation with God, that's it. Humans like to make things more difficult than they truly are; I believe it is because it makes us feel important—compared to a simple way to communicate with Father. Prayer is simply talking with God. Just like you share different things with the people in your life; you do not always come to God the same way. And He does not always answer you the way He did before. You may need a time of weeping and tears during a wilderness season or painful time with Him. You may be going through some things you cannot understand, and you are frustrated. You may feel anger at a situation in your life—tell Him, just like you would a family member or friend. Be honest with God, He already knows, anyway; that is what prayer is all about! After you share your "prayers" with Him—stop and then listen to His response.

Many may say to me, "I talk to God, but He does not talk back. I do not know when He is speaking to me. I do not hear Him." Like any relationship, it takes time to know the voice of the one you are spending time with; like your spouse; you hear them, but it takes time to truly understand what they are saying and how they are replying or relating to you. It is like a light bulb comes on and you say, "I heard you, Lord! I know how You speak to me." That does not mean God will talk with you the same way all the time—He can choose to talk with you any way He desires. Be open. Once you hear Him, though, you will begin to hear Him more and more! To hear one talk with you, (not to you or at you) you must be quiet and let them talk. It is God's desire to respond to you in a conversation with you - let Him talk with you - not just you talking to Him. Remember, Enoch walked with God. Enoch let God lead him, not the other way around. It is important in your relationship with God, to allow Him time to talk with you. I practice soaking in His Holy Spirit; that is resting in Him, without speaking much to Him. Sometimes we sit together and I rest in Him and let Him share with me His desires for me, instead of me doing all the talking and telling Him what I want. This is another book, too - soaking and resting in Him.

I remember, as a very young Christian, I was returning to my seat in church after going up to the altar for a special offering. As I walked, I asked the Lord, "Lord, how do I know if I am prophetic?" I no sooner arrived at my seat and the lady in front of me says, "Brenda, you are prophetic. You have the prophetic gifting. I am not saying you are a prophet. You are prophetic." Wow! That is my relationship with Father. I speak with Him like I do if I were talking with you. Another time I was in worship (that is when Holy Spirit loves to talk with me) and I received a picture in my head. I saw a banquet table filled with food and the Lord spoke to me with one sentence, "I have prepared a table for My children, come and eat." I felt this was the Spirit of the Lord speaking to me and I knew the word was a corporate word for the body of Christ. I was unsure if this was me or the Lord, so I asked the Lord, I said, "If this is You, Lord, then have Pastor Ronnie say, 'Brenda has a word for the church,' or 'A woman has a word for the church.'" Well, within minutes Pastor Ronnie said, "There is a woman in the church who has a word for the body. Come quickly!" I about fell out right there! And I was standing! I ran up and delivered the word from God. It was exhilarating and scary all at the same time. I allowed Holy Spirit to speak through me to His body for the first time in my life.

Do not be afraid to ask God for whatever you need to help you be all He has called you to be! Father knew I was in reverence of Him. I did not want to go up and give a word in my own strength or ability. That was my starting point. I learned how Holy Spirit speaks with me at the beginning. Now He speaks to me different ways, dreams, visions, sounds, nature, etc., and yet, we still have the intimate relationship of communication with one another! I love Him so very much and I know He loves me and wants to spend time with me!

If you have never soaked or rested in Him, I encourage you to take this time to stop and rest in Christ—rest in Holy Spirit—rest in Father. For just a few minutes, stop and close your eyes. Do not seek the Lord for anything, except Him — His Presence. The amount of time you spend is not important at first. All that is important is that you stop and rest in Him. Listen for Him to speak to you.

Chapter Six

God's Word is truth, not truth based on man's vision; the Word of God is absolute Truth, it cannot be moved or changed, just because man says different than God. God loves to reveal His truth to His people. God wants us to know Him and His plans. It is up to us to search His holy Scriptures for what He is saying and what He expects from us, after we receive the knowledge He shares. Let us look at and discuss a few scriptures that give us a hint of things to come. The prophetic is the future, yes; it is all about what is happening right before your eyes. We carry an authority in the spirit realm and that authority circumvents the lies of the enemy and breaks through the spirit realm into the natural realm, making a difference not only in your spirit for you individually, but also on earth! The same authority in Christ is in us! Open your eyes to see what Christ has done!

King David knew the authority he had; that is obvious in the Scriptures.

> But David said to Saul, 'Your servant used to keep his father's sheep, and when a lion or a bear came and took a lamb out of the flock, I went out after it and struck it, and delivered the lamb from its mouth; and when it arose against me, I caught it by its beard, and struck and killed it. Your servant has killed both lion and bear; and this uncircumcised Philistine will be like one of them, seeing he has defied the armies of the living God." Moreover David

said, "The LORD, who delivered me from the paw of the lion and from the paw of the bear, He will deliver me from the hand of this Philistine." And Saul said to David, "Go, and the LORD be with you! Then David said to the Philistine, 'You come to me with a sword, with a spear, and with a javelin. But I come to you in the name of the LORD of hosts, the God of the armies of Israel, whom you have defied.'"

1 Samuel 17: 34-37, 45

David proceeded to tell the enemy what he was going to do, just like the enemy had told the Israelites what he was going to do to them. He spoke the future into existence by his words of faith! The shepherd David knew who he was and what he could do in the power of his Lord, and since he had already killed lions and bears in the wilderness, David knew the Lord his God was with him. David was not capable of killing a lion and a bear on his own, in his own strength. He stated the Lord delivered him from the lion and the bear and now his Lord would deliver him from this Philistine. David looked at this Philistine as he did at the lion and the bear—as an enemy to defeat. He knew what God was able to do and he trusted the word of the Lord and his authority! David did not trust himself, He trusted the LORD! He trusted God, because when he was in the wilderness alone, only God was with him and only God delivered him. David knew he could defeat the enemy in the NAME OF THE LORD, not in his own name.

Prophetically, as he did many times as king, David spoke into his future by the word of the Lord. He did not let "what he saw" deter him from what his purpose and place was in the heavens and on this earth. Was he thinking about all that?

Probably not, more than likely he was just being David, a man filled with faith in his God. David already knew what God was capable to do in any battle; he had seen the Lord move on his behalf in the wilderness.

The wilderness is the place to grow your faith. In your daily times, the times when no one else is around, the time when no one sees but God; that is when your faith is increasing through the circumstances, through the words you speak to the situation. The time you spend with God changes your perception of self. You begin to see and recognize the man or woman God sees in you.

In the New Testament, we consistently read how many people came to Jesus and they were healed or delivered, or whatever it was they needed was done for them "in the NAME OF JESUS." The power of the Name of Jesus will overcome everything that stands in your way, everything that keeps you from being all you are in Him. After this battle David was brought to Saul and he remained with Saul. His destiny was open before his very eyes. (Prior to this David was anointed king; see 1 Samuel 16:13.) David was anointed king, yet he did not immediately walk into his called place. After his faith and authority persevered over Goliath, God moved him one step closer to his destiny as king, and brought him before King Saul.

Everything you go through reflects who you are in God's perfect will on this earth. During some tough or painful times, we are too quick to stop the process of understanding Who God is and what He is doing with us during that season. Everything is to prepare us for Him—His purposes for us! It is time for the body to step out in faith and authority and move in God's will on earth as it is in heaven! (See Matthew 6: 10; Luke 11: 2.)

"Those who see you will gaze at you, and consider you, saying: 'Is this the man who made the earth tremble, who shook kingdoms, who made the world as a wilderness and destroyed its cities, who did not open the house of his prisoners?'" (Isaiah 14:16-17)

When we see the enemy, Satan, we will see the truth of who he is and what he is. His defeat happened years ago on the cross and even though he has power, once again I reiterate, he has no authority to use the power he has against us, the body of Christ. Satan is the greatest illusionist, ever. He is filled with lies. He is not capable to speaking truth. He is the father of lies. (See John 8:44.)

> Behold, I give you the authority to trample on serpents and scorpions, and over all the power of the enemy, and nothing shall by any means hurt you. Nevertheless do not rejoice in this, that the spirits are subject to you, but rather rejoice because your names are written in heaven.
>
> Luke 10:19- 20

"Serpents" in this verse is the Greek word *ophis* (*o'-fĕs*) meaning, "a snake; with the ancients, the serpent was an emblem of cunning and wisdom."[13] The serpent who deceived Eve was regarded by the Jews as the devil (*Blue Letter Bible*). The word in Greek for "scorpions" is *skorpios* (*skor-pĕ'-os*)[14] which means just what we imagine: "a scorpion, the name of a little animal, somewhat resembling a lobster, which in warm regions lurk, esp. in stone walls; it has a poisonous sting in its tail." It

---

13   Strong's Concordance
14   Strong's Concordance

is possible it comes from a root meaning "to pierce." (*Blue Letter Bible*). *Vine's* states, regarding scorpion: "Lord's assurance to the disciples of the authority given them by Him to tread upon serpents and scorpions conveys the thought of victory over spiritually antagonistic forces, the powers of darkness." It is clear to see in the words of Christ that we are victorious over the enemy and all his cunning lies. We are victorious over ALL his power. The next verse in Luke 10, that is verse 21, says, "In that hour Jesus rejoiced in the Spirit and said, 'I thank You, Father, Lord of heaven and earth, that You have hidden these things from the wise and prudent and revealed them to babes. Even so, Father, for so it seemed good in Your sight'" (Luke 10:21).

After He makes this bold statement regarding the power and authority we have been given and the loss of the enemy's power, Jesus rejoices. "Rejoice" in this verse is the Greek word *chairō* (*khī'-rō*) meaning: "be glad; to rejoice exceedingly."[15] Many believe the word reveals Jesus' joy that we will be with Him in heaven. He dances and rejoices because we are with Him. Jesus was more joyous over the truth that we will be with Him eternally, than the truth that we have authority over the power of the enemy. Do we have the same mindset? Or have we been so deterred by the lies of the enemy, we focus on the enemy and not Christ?

In reading these verses it appears to me Jesus was saying, matter-of-factly, that we are victorious, and that is awesome! Yet, He was much more excited about this truth: We will be with Him eternally! Jesus says the things God has chosen to reveal to us, His body. He conceals these truths from the wise and prudent of this world. You know something the world

---

15 Strong's Concordance

does not. You are "in the know" of the things of God. You are on the inside looking out!

"Forever, O LORD, Your word is settled in heaven" (Psalm 119:89).

"Tremble before Him, all the earth. The world also is firmly established, It shall not be moved" (1 Chronicles 16:30).

God's word is settled (stands) in heaven; it is established (standing or erect) and cannot or will not be removed in His abode, heaven. God's word is the same here on earth when we speak it by faith! By faith we press in and make a difference in our lives here in this realm.

When God wanted to make a change in someone's life here on earth, often He would change their name. Why? So they would get an understanding of who they were in Him. God already knows who they are and what they are capable of to complete His perfect will. For instance, God changed Abram's name (exalted father) to Abraham (father of a multitude or chief of a multitude). (See Genesis 17:5.) God already knew who Abraham was and his destiny in Him. The kicker was this, Abram did not know who he was. God spoke his future in the new name He gave him. God changed Sarai's (chief, governor, leader, in the masculine form) name to Sarah (princess/noblewoman). (See Genesis 17:15.) When God changed their names, He not only spoke their future, He gave them the grace to walk into their future. "Abram" is now "Abraham," and "Sarai" is now "Sarah." God added the "heh" in the Hebrew language; Abram had it added to the middle of his name, while Sarai had it added to the end of her name.

Let's look at what God was doing. God visited Abram five times and it was on the fifth visit God changed his name to Abraham. Five is the number of grace. "Heh" is the fifth letter in the Hebrew alphabet, representing grace; and it also represents YHVH Elohim. When He added this letter to the middle of "Abram," God was relaying to Abram, I AM now in the middle of all your circumstances and I AM in the midst of wherever you are. Adding this Hebrew letter to the end of "Sarai," God changed her name from a masculine (men cannot bear children) to a female form meaning the "feminine ideal of gentleness, loving affection and devotion." Females can bear children, while the masculine cannot. The addition of the Hebrew letter "heh" turned their lives completely around. Also, as a note, the first time we read and hear the name El Shaddai, "Almighty God, or the multi-breasted One," is in Genesis 17 when God begins to speak to Abram, just before He changes his name.

"When Abram was ninety-nine years old, the LORD appeared to Abram and said to him, "I am Almighty God; walk before Me and be blameless" (Genesis 17:1). "Almighty God" is the Hebrew title, "EL Shaddai." How can we believe the God we serve is a God Who is not interested inner daily lives? My Jesus! There are others who's names God changed: "Jacob" was changed to "Israel." (See Genesis 32:28.) And in the New Testament Christ changed Simon's name to "Peter." (See John 1:42.)

When God speaks of the "name of Jesus" or the "name of the Lord," He is speaking about the character of that persona. We have been taught if we just "name it and claim it," things will happen. No, it isn't just speaking the word—it is knowing the Word—that is Christ.

"In the beginning the Word and the Word was with God and the Word was God" (John 1:1). Jesus is the Word of God manifest on this earth. Anyone can speak words, but when you know, that is experience, the One of whom you speak, everything changes! Once Abraham and Sarah had new names, they were able to experience God in a new way. They had a revelation of Him they had not seen before. Even though the future did not manifest immediately, their future was set, ready for God to move in His timing.

Have you had a revelation of God? I am talking about true experiences with Father? Do you want your name changed? In other words, are you prepared to walk out of who you are today into who God ordained you to be before the foundations of the world? Abram moved into a new realm when his name changed, yet it was twenty-five years before the promise came forth; that is Isaac. Every time the name "Abraham" was spoken, his future came closer to this realm!

Abraham's faith was his continued walk with God, every step of the way, as he waited for the promise to manifest. He believed, no matter how long it took! He continued to pull from the spirit realm, by being with God and looking past his earthly place and into the realm of God!

Chapter Seven

God changed the names of some of the greatest people in His Word. God has changed all our names, at least our last name. We have been adopted and now are in a new family in heaven. We now are a different creation in Christ, actually, we are a new creation (continually transforming to be like Christ). Our names say much about us. What does your name mean? When you were born, what was the name your parents gave you—your God-given name?

My mom was going to call me "Peggy." I was born in the 1950s. "Peggy Sue" was a very popular song during that era. When it came time to name me, she called me "Brenda." Yay! I am glad. I like the name "Brenda" and it fits me. The name "Brenda" means, "sword or torch." I am both, strong, cutting like the sword of truth in the Word of God in Hebrews 4:12, and a torch, as in Genesis 15:17, a light or flame, guiding people to the Truth, Jesus. I am a strong woman in the spirit realm and in the natural. The characteristics God gave me flow together for His glory.

The sword is a weapon in the natural, and it is a weapon in the spirit—the Word of God is a sword. I speak the Word of God with conviction and truth. I am not afraid to stand for the Word of God. As a prophetess, I have to be strong and I must be a light, guiding people to the truth in Christ. Unfortunately, because I am strong, many people in the Body of Christ are intimidated by my presence and confidence in Christ. I will say this, with as much grace as I can, I am not concerned with what anyone else thinks of me. I know who I am in my Savior.

I embrace who I am in Christ. I love me. I love who God created me to be.

It is not by chance God told me to name the ministry He gave me to steward "Radical Fire Ministries." I do not believe in coincidences in Christ. I believe God has ordained each and every day for me and He has prepared my way. The name He gave me describes me spiritually and naturally. I walk in who I am, who I have been called to be. The word "radical" means "original." In other words, our ministry could be called "Original Fire Ministries." This is His fire from heaven, not man-made fire. This is the fire that comes down from heaven and burns the living sacrifice! He is the fire, the flame, the torch. He is the sword. I am only part of Who and What He is.

In Judges 6, we meet a man called "Gideon." Gideon was named for his purpose and destiny, in his time, just like I am in my time. Before we discuss Gideon, I would like to give us a backdrop of what was going on in Israel prior to Gideon coming on the scene. I will paraphrase the first ten verses in chapter six.

The beginning of Judges 6 tells how Israel had been disobedient to the Lord and did evil in His sight; therefore, the Lord delivered them into the hands of the people of Midian. Whenever it was time for the harvest, the Midianites would come and destroy the land. They would steal and destroy not only the crops, but the livestock as well. So the Israelites were impoverished, they were in lack, naturally and spiritually. Finally, they cried out to the Lord and he answered them through a prophet. The prophet spoke the word of the Lord and told them God had delivered them, brought them out of bondage and still they disobeyed Him. This brings us to verse 11, where we see an Angel of the Lord comes and visits a man, Gideon.

In this verse, Gideon is threshing wheat in a winepress, hiding, because of the oppression of the Midianites. It appears as though Gideon is afraid of the Midianites. Now, it is time for God to intervene and change Israelite's the circumstances and He plans on using Gideon, the one who is in fear.

"And the Angel of the Lord appeared to him, and said to him, 'The LORD is with you, you mighty man of valor!'" (Judges 6: 12).

Mighty man of valor? Who is the Angel of the Lord talking about? Gideon? Hmmm, Gideon, yes, the angel is addressing Gideon. In Hebrew "Gideon" means, "hewer or warrior; with the root of the name meaning to cut, chop down, destroy anything."[16]

God is speaking to Gideon as WHO he is—not who he thinks he is. God speaks out the truth when He calls on the name of Gideon. The angel said, "man of valor!" Gideon did not look like a man of valor, nor did he think like one or feel like one. In verse 13, Gideon asks the angel why all this is happening, where is the God Who brought them out of bondage by miracles, signs, and wonders? It is always amazing to me how when the people in the Bible asked God questions, He very rarely answers them directly. Instead, He speaks to them prophetically, that is how He sees everything. God sees from a different perspective than we see.

Now the angel is no longer talking, but the LORD is talking directly, "Then the Lord turned to him and said, 'Go in this might of yours, and you shall save Israel from the hand of the Midianites. Have I not sent you?'" (Judges 6: 14).

God does not answer Gideon's questions, instead, He speaks truth from His perspective. What He says is the truth

---

[16] Strong's Concordance

of who Gideon is and what he will do following the Lord and His instructions. Again, the conversation from Gideon's lips is all about what he knows and sees in the natural. Gideon tells the Lord how weak his tribe is and how he is the weakest of them all. But God continues to respond to Gideon with His version of what He sees. "And the Lord said to him, 'Surely I will be with you, and you shall defeat the Midianites as one man.'" (Judges 6:16).

One man? Me? Do you wonder what is going through the mind of the Mighty Man of Valor, this Warrior of God? Something has shifted, Gideon's thinking seems to be moving toward the thinking of God. "Then he said to Him, 'If now I have found favor in Your sight, then show me a sign that it is You who talk with me.'" (Judges 16:17).

Gideon needs something tangible to hold on to, something to help him understand what is happening here. Is he really talking with the Angel of God and with God Himself? The Lord agrees to be part of what Gideon needs to increase his faith. God did not condemn or reprimand Gideon, no, God understands where we are in our walk with Him. He knows what it will take to get you to the place of great faith, a place where there is no doubt in your words.

Gideon wanted to give an offering to the Lord, and God allowed Him to do so. (Read Judges 6:19-24.) God knows just what to say, at any given moment in your life, to move you to the next place in faith. According to verse 22 Gideon "perceived" it was the Angel of the Lord who spoke to him and he built an altar to the Lord. The Lord told him in verse 23, "Peace be with you; do not fear, you shall not die" (Judges 6:23).

Then the Lord tells Gideon, "I want you to do something for me, now, tear down the altar of Ba'al. (See verse 25.) There is a beginning to this Mighty Man of Valor. He is instructed to do something after God proves to him, "I AM with you." And even though Gideon is fearful and concerned for his life, he obeys the Lord's instructions, and by night he takes ten men with him and tears down the altars of Ba'al. No matter how or when he did it, Gideon did it. He began to step out on the faith God had deposited in Him through their conversations!

God continued to press Gideon to do what was necessary to complete the task first given him, which was defeating the Midianites. The first step was to tear down their places of worship. Their power was to be removed! I am not sure if Gideon understood the authority it took in the spirit realm to do what he did in the natural realm. Once the altar was torn down the enemy did not have an "opening" to enter! From that moment on, things changed for Gideon. He was beginning see himself as God saw him. This is a good read for those who have been told they have a purpose and a place in the kingdom of God, but they are not sure if they believe the word given them by the Lord, be it a direct word, or a word from a prophet or prophetess.

Gideon's task was not complete. Remember, he was to take Israel back from the hands of the Midianites. (See verse 14.) Gideon decided it was time to test the Lord and be sure God had truly chosen him for this task. In Judges 6:36-40, Gideon continues with the only way he knows to increase his faith. He tells the Lord, "If You have chosen me for this and I am the one to deliver Israel from the hands of the enemy, then do this one thing; I will put a piece of wool on the threshing floor and if the dew is only on the wool in the morning, I know you have chosen me." And it was as Gideon had asked. In the morning the dew was only on the wool. (See verses 37 and 38.) And still

Gideon needed encouragement! So He asked God to do the opposite; put dew on the ground and leave the wool dry; and the next morning it was as Gideon had spoken.

Do you see how the conversations with God increased Gideon's faith? Do you see Gideon moving from fear to faith? Gideon is not afraid to ask God for a sign, for his faith was as weak as his tribe (in his eyes), and yet, after conversations with God, and a deed done in the natural, Gideon began to shift his gaze from himself to his God!

When we are asked to do something for God, it is okay to ask Him for a sign. God is okay with our questions, as long as there is action, too. Gideon was told to begin the actual task of delivering Israel by going to the Midianites camp. Judges 7:9-11, states that Gideon was told to go to the camp, for God had given him the Midianites. But if he was afraid (which God knew he was) God told him to bring his servant, Purah, with him. God told Gideon, "You will hear what they say and know I have given you the strength to complete your assignment." (All of this is paraphrased, of course. Please read this chapter in full to get a thorough understanding of how Gideon went from fear to faith.)

To give a shortened version of this story, Gideon and his servant, Purah, went to the camp and overheard some of the men talking about a dream and the interpretation of that dream. They deduced the dream meant the Midianites would lose at the hands of the Israelites. The Midianites said, "God has delivered Midian and the whole camp" (verse 14).

"And so it was, when Gideon heard the telling of the dream and its interpretation, that he worshiped. He returned to the camp of Israel, and said, 'Arise, for the Lord has delivered the camp of Midian into your hand'" (Judges 7:15).

Gideon heard the Midianites speaking the same words God spoke to him and it increased his faith all the more! The enemy knew Gideon would be successful, even when Gideon did not! What a mighty God we serve! He gave ears to hear and eyes to see what the Spirit of the Lord is saying and doing. And yes, Gideon and his three hundred men took the Midianites and the Amalekites by the power of the Lord and Gideon's faith in the Lord. Gideon was not afraid to check and double check to be sure he was hearing from the Lord, not a different spirit, to make sure he could complete the task given.

What is the task, or the calling on your life? Do you know? If you know, are you walking with God to make His destiny for you come to pass? Think about this last chapter and seek God for His direction in your life. Do not be discouraged if you research your name and do not like what it means. Ask God to change it. Do not be afraid to talk with God and walk with God. He loves you and wants the best for you. Believe that word.

Chapter Eight

There is a woman in the Scripture who has always intrigued me. This woman's faith blows me out of the water. She is intelligent, bold, and filled with faith that will bring the spiritual realm into the natural realm right before her eyes.

> Now it happened one day that Elisha went to Shunem, where there was a notable woman, and she persuaded him to eat some food. So it was, as often as he passed by, he would turn in there to eat some food. And she said to her husband, "Look now, I know that this is a holy man of God, who passes by us regularly. Please, let us make a small upper room on the wall; and let us put a bed for him there, and a table and a chair and a lampstand; so it will be, whenever he comes to us, he can turn in there."
> And it happened one day that he came there, and he turned in to the upper room and lay down there. Then he said to Gehazi his servant, "Call this Shunammite woman." When he had called her, she stood before him. And he said to him, "Say now to her, 'Look, you have been concerned for us with all this care. What can I do for you? Do you want me to speak on your behalf to the king or to the commander of the army?'"
> She answered, "I dwell among my own people."
> So he said, "What then is to be done for her?" And Gehazi answered, "Actually, she has no son, and her

husband is old."

So he said, "Call her." When he had called her, she stood in the doorway. Then he said, "About this time next year you shall embrace a son."

And she said, "No, my lord. Man of God, do not lie to your maidservant!"

But the woman conceived, and bore a son when the appointed time had come, of which Elisha had told her.

And the child grew. Now it happened one day that he went out to his father, to the reapers. And he said to his father, "My head, my head!"

So he said to a servant, "Carry him to his mother." When he had taken him and brought him to his mother, he sat on her knees till noon, and then died. And she went up and laid him on the bed of the man of God, shut the door upon him, and went out. Then she called to her husband, and said, "Please send me one of the young men and one of the donkeys, that I may run to the man of God and come back."

So he said, "Why are you going to him today? It is neither the New Moon nor the Sabbath."

And she said, "It is well." Then she saddled a donkey, and said to her servant, "Drive, and go forward; do not slacken the pace for me unless I tell you." And so she departed, and went to the man of God at Mount Carmel.

So it was, when the man of God saw her afar off, that he said to his servant Gehazi, "Look, the Shunammite woman! Please run now to meet her, and say to her, 'Is it well with you? Is it well with your husband? Is it well with the child?'"

And she answered, "It is well." Now when she came to the man of God at the hill, she caught him by the feet, but Gehazi came near to push her away. But the man of God said, "Let her alone; for her soul is in deep distress, and the Lord has hidden it from me, and has not told me."

So she said, "Did I ask a son of my lord? Did I not say, 'Do not deceive me'?"

Then he said to Gehazi, "Get yourself ready, and take my staff in your hand, and be on your way. If you meet anyone, do not greet him; and if anyone greets you, do not answer him; but lay my staff on the face of the child."

And the mother of the child said, "As the Lord lives, and as your soul lives, I will not leave you." So he arose and followed her. Now Gehazi went on ahead of them, and laid the staff on the face of the child; but there was neither voice nor hearing. Therefore he went back to meet him, and told him, saying, "The child has not awakened."

When Elisha came into the house, there was the child, lying dead on his bed. He went in therefore, shut the door behind the two of them, and prayed to the Lord. And he went up and lay on the child, and put his mouth on his mouth, his eyes on his eyes, and his hands on his hands; and he stretched himself out on the child, and the flesh of the child became warm. He returned and walked back and forth in the house, and again went up and stretched himself out on him; then the child sneezed seven times, and the child opened his eyes. And he called Gehazi and said, "Call this Shunammite woman." So he called her. And when she came in to him, he said, "Pick up your son." So she went in, fell at his feet, and bowed to the ground; then she picked up her son and went out.

2 Kings 4:8-37

This woman's faith is amazing, even though it is not described as great faith; in fact the word "faith" is not even mentioned in this scripture. And yet, her faith, I describe as explosive. This woman was a notable woman, a noble woman. She was more than likely a wealthy woman who was content with the life she lived in the town of Shunem, a town in the tribe of Issachar. Issachar is the tribe of Israel that knew the signs of the times and the seasons. When God has a miracle for you, there is always an appointed time for that miracle to manifest. In this scripture we see her serving and expecting nothing in return; she was not serving to receive her desire, which we know is to have a son; she was serving because it pleased her to do so.

> Yet it shall not be so among you; but whoever desires to become great among you shall be your servant. And whoever of you desires to be first shall be slave of all. For even the Son of Man did not come to be served, but to serve, and to give His life a ransom for many.
>
> Mark 10:43-45

Her faith was not "faith" because she wanted something; her "faith" was only to serve. Serving is a concept that is missing in the body of Christ today; serve just to serve, because serving in itself is rewarding. In the Old Testament it was not like the New Testament, they did not have direct access to God; therefore they served the prophets, as they would God. Because of her heart to serve the man of God he reached out to her and asked her what he may do for her. Speak to the king on her behalf? This awesome woman said, "There is nothing I need, I am satisfied with where I am and what I have." Then the servant of Elisha, Gehazi, told Elisha, "The woman has no children, no son, no heir."

Elisha, the prophet, did not know everything. He did not know what her deepest desire was. He did not know what to ask the Lord for on her behalf. Prophets only know what God shares with them. We, the body of Christ, must stop assuming prophets are all knowing, they are not. Only God knows all and when He chooses to share, then (and only then) does a true prophet speak! It was after the prophet found out she had no children; he called her back where he and his servant were waiting—a doorway now opened. Verse 15 says, "So he (Elisha) said, 'Call her.' When he had called her, she stood in the doorway."

What doorway? The natural doorway to Elisha and the spiritual doorway to the miracles of God. Remember, she is in the town of the people of Issachar. They knew the signs and seasons; not the seasons of man, but of God. The meaning for "doorway" in the Hebrew language is "opening, entrance"— the root word means, "to let loose, be open, thrown open, loose oneself, to loose open oneself."[17] It was time for her blessing to

---

17   Strong's Concordance

come to pass. She was in the right place at the right time and now everything lined up according to God's plan and purpose. The prophet told her she would conceive and "about this time next year you will hold your son." In verse 17 it says she conceived and had a son "when the appointed time had come."

The "appointed time" phrase is the Hebrew word `*eth (āth)*. This word means it is "the proper time or due season." The root for this word is `*ad (ad)*. This word means "perpetuity, forever, continuing future."[18] Continuing future was in her; all she had to do was come to the door that was opened for her and walk through. In John 10:9, Christ states that He is the Door, the Resurrection and Life! It is in Him that your future exists and is released! Christ is the Door. The promise is in the Promiser—Christ! Now the miracle had manifested, and everything was fine, for a time.

After some years, this young boy was helping his father in the fields and became ill. Some theologians say it could have been heatstroke. I do not know what happened physically. What I do know is this woman's son died from some physical ailment. She was devastated, I am sure. Here is her young son, the promise from God before her very eyes, dead! As a mother, I can imagine what went through her mind, and yet, the word says she did not speak what she saw. This woman spoke what she wanted, what was to be. The prophet spoke and it came to pass. She bore a son and he was her heir. We must "see" her faith by her words and her actions.

"But do you want to know, O foolish man, that faith without works is dead?" (James 2:20).

"For as the body without the spirit is dead, so faith without works is dead also" (James 2:26).

---

18   Strong's Concordance

This woman decided how she was going to react to what happened to her son. When her son died, she put him in the room where the man of God had stayed. All she knew to do was to go to the one who spoke over her, the one whom she served. She laid her son in the bed, the place of rest for Elisha. Men and woman who truly follow God, and serve Him, carry an anointing. This anointing can be felt, like the presence of God. She laid her son upon the bed where the prophet, Elisha, had been; where the anointing rested. Her actions spoke more than any words could speak. She was not prepared to let go of her promise.

This woman's son was dead; her promise from God had died. And yet, when she saw that her son was no longer living; she laid him on the bed of the prophet and went out to find the man of God. She did not call her best friend and speak the fact that her son was dead. She did not call her husband, crying, and agree with him that their son was dead. This awesome woman of faith did not weep and wail to the heavens! What this woman did and said says it all. She laid the boy on the bed then went out and called to her husband, asking him to ready a servant and a donkey for her journey to the man of God. As you are reading this scripture (re-read verse 22), she says, as I paraphrase: "I am going to the man of God and I am returning." And her husband's response was so "church" typical. He says in verse 23, "'Why are you going to him today? It is neither the New Moon nor the Sabbath.' And she said, 'All is well.'"

She gets a typical church response from her husband. "Why are you dealing with the man of God? It is neither Sunday nor Wednesday; why are you going to church today?" In other words, why spend more time in the house of God, with the man of God, or in the presence of God than is required? Required by whom? Religion! This woman was not interested in religion, she was interested in God. Her answer is a response of phenomenal faith! "All is well." What? All is well? According to what I see, nothing is well. Her son is dead and yet, she does not say that! She says what her faith commands her to say. She does not look at the circumstance as it is, but as it is in faith, in the realm of God. She did not speak what was, she only spoke what she wanted to be! Remember in the Old Testament, this was her way of going to God, to see the man of God. He was the one who spoke the miracle, her son, into existence. She could not get to him fast enough. She saddled her own donkey and told her servant, We stop for no-one or no thing. All is well."

No matter your dream, it still lives as long as you are alive. Your dream lives as long as you have breath in your body. I want to remind you—when God speaks to you: His word will not return to Him void of power, it will go forth and accomplish what He sent it to do. (See Isaiah 55:11.) No one, not even the enemy, can take what God has said from you. His promises are yours. In Christ they are "Yes and amen." God's word is established in heaven! His word is more powerful and more real than the world you see. Believing that is faith!

The Word tell us she ran to Elisha, she wasted no time in getting to him at Mt. Carmel. Mt. Carmel is the same place Elijah (Elisha's teacher) confronted the prophets of Ba'al, the prophets of Ahab and Jezebel. Mt. Carmel was the place the enemy was confronted and defeated. Mt. Carmel's meaning in Hebrew is "fruitful; plentiful; a place cultivated as a garden, planted with fruit trees and herbs, a garden land," and the root means, "a vineyard."[19] Jesus said, "I am the true vine, and My Father is the vinedresser. I am the vine, you are the branches. He who abides in Me, and I in him, bears much fruit; for without Me you can do nothing" (John 15:1,5).

This awesome woman's faith was headed to the place where the man of God was, the vineyard, a place of fertile ground. A place where faith grows in Christ!

Elisha saw this woman coming from afar and he sent his servant, Gehazi, to meet her and ask her, "Is it well with you? Is it well with your husband? Is it well with your son?" And once again her response was by faith: "It is well." When she came before the man of God, she fell at his feet in a worship position. Again I want to reiterate, the prophet did not know what had happened with this woman and her son. Prophets ONLY know what God shares with them. Even Elijah says in verse 27, "… the Lord has hidden it from me, and has not told me." Just because we are prophets, or prophetic people, does not mean we know everything. Only God knows everything and He chooses when and what to share in His timing.

In her distress, she spoke her complaint: "Did I ask for a son? Didn't I say 'Do not deceive me?'" In other words, she questioned why the child was given and then taken away. I did not ask for this dream, but you gave it to me in your grace. Why take it now? Why did you speak a thing and then allow the thing to die? Her faith could not be shaken. She stayed with the man of God and would not leave his side. She was not going to let him out of her sight. She was ready to receive the continuation of her miracle. Her dream would live again! It would not die! Her son would live again; that is what her faith was speaking to her. The man of God came and resur-

---

19   Strong's Concordance

rected her son, her dream, her miracle! Once again he lived! Before she went to her son, the first thing she did was lay at the feet of Elisha once again. Her position in her faith was always worship; her eyes were always on the ONE who produced the miracle, that is God! She was not worshipping the man; she worshipped God, the ONE who brought the man who spoke the word of the Lord.

Faith is not just words, it is also action. When you tell God you believe, show Him you believe. Do what is necessary to reveal to Him your faith. What is it you are believing for from God? Where is the action of your faith? If you are believing for a new job, are you putting in applications as you are led by Holy Spirit? If you are asking God for a closer walk with Him, are you reading His word? Are you praying? Are you doing anything, by faith, to show God your heart? God already knows, but there is something about taking a step forward that pleases Father and He moves on your behalf.

In the fall of 2018, my husband, Windell, made a decision to change his eating habits and adopt a healthly lifestyle. He has worked all his life, but his lifestyle was sedentary. He did not eat healthy food or portions (I am a great cook). He wanted change—he was overweight, so he made little changes at first. He stopped drinking soda and quit eating bread in the months of November and December. He was taking action, not just speaking words, but he was doing something about his weight. I was praying and sharing with the Lord that when we could, I would like to have a "personal trainer," someone to help us get started with better health and understanding of our bodies. I saw an ad in a magazine for a gym in Georgetown, Texas called GETAGEFIT; this is specifically for people age 50+. GETAGEFIT was having a drawing for a free eight-week VIP membership, around Christmas time. The VIP membership included 16 sessions with a personal trainer, 4 sessions with a nutritionist, and 1 session with a meal planner. I went to the gym and entered the contest! My husband won the drawing! Praise be to God!

In the first week of January 2019, we were at the gym and making an effort to change our lifestyle. My husband and I talked later and we believe God blessed us with winning the drawing, because my husband had already begun to walk in faith with his actions by making changes before our prayer was answered. He did not wait until he won to begin making changes, he began and then God moved! By the way, Theo T., the founder of GETAGEFIT and Kelly M., our personal trainer, are the best. Theo and Kelly continually encourage us and push us to another level. If you're ever in Georgetown please stop by and say, "Hi." Tell them Brenda Eagans sent you!

Faith is believing something BEFORE you see it. If you see it first, where is the faith in that? It is time for the Body of Christ to stop waiting on God to move for them, before they move toward Him. This is the time and season God is releasing more than ever to His Bride, do not be the one with a lamp but no oil. (See Matthew 25:1-13.) Move out on faith and watch the King of kings fill your lamp right before your eyes. Step out into your calling. Your purpose for His glory is waiting to meet you and engulf you in His love!

Chapter Nine

In the Body of Christ, Hebrews 11 is known as the "hall of faith." The unknown author speaks of the men and women who went before us and their faith in God and His promises. The author writes about Abel, and his faith in offering a more excellent sacrifice than his brother Cain. There is Enoch, who pleased God so much, God took Him. He just disappeared from this earth and we assume he was taken to heaven with His Father. Hebrews 11 speaks of Abraham and Sarah, the mother and father of the Hebrew people, and their faith to believe for the promise of God, no matter how old their bodies were. The man, Noah, is also mentioned in this faith chapter.

"By faith Noah, being divinely warned of things not yet seen, moved with godly fear, prepared an ark for the saving of his household, by which he condemned the world and became heir of the righteousness which is according to faith" (Hebrews 11:7).

Did you get that? I hope so. God spoke the sentence, and yet, the Word says Noah was the one who condemned the world because of his faith and obedience to God. Noah put action to the word spoken over him because of his faith and obedience. Noah condemned the world. "Condemned" in this verse means, "to give judgment against, to judge worthy of punishment, to sentence."[20] God was saying Noah completed the sentence of God to the people, by his faith and action while building the ark. God spoke to Noah and Noah agreed with God.

---

20   Strong's Concordance

It is almost impossible for me to comprehend this Scripture, knowing that our actions in faith can condemn or save, depending on God's planned outcome for the circumstance. Do we truly understand the implications of the words we speak and the actions we take? What if Noah would have taken no action? What if there was no one saved, and God decided to re-recreate man?

God speaks a word and His will is a "man" hears the word and acts on the word. It is up to us to act on the word given to us by Holy Spirit. In Ezekiel 3 we see the prophet is told what happens when God speaks to him and he does not give the word God has spoken.

> Now it came to pass at the end of seven days that the word of the Lord came to me, saying, "Son of man, I have made you a watchman for the house of Israel; therefore hear a word from My mouth, and give them warning from Me: When I say to the wicked, 'You shall surely die,' and you give him no warning, nor speak to warn the wicked from his wicked way, to save his life, that same wicked man shall die in his iniquity; but his blood I will require at your hand. Yet, if you warn the wicked, and he does not turn from his wickedness, nor from his wicked way, he shall die in his iniquity; but you have delivered your soul. Again, when a righteous man turns from his righteousness and commits iniquity, and I lay a stumbling block before him, he shall die; because you did not give him warning, he shall die in his sin, and his righteousness which he has done shall not be remembered; but his blood I

will require at your hand. Nevertheless if you warn the righteous man that the righteous should not sin, and he does not sin, he shall surely live because he took warning; also you will have delivered your soul.

Ezekiel 3:16-21

Ezekiel is told his blood will be required if he does not speak the word of the Lord to the one God has chosen. God has a plan and purpose for each and every one of us—it is up to us, when a word is spoken, to deliver that word or take whatever action God has spoken so that we will not be required to pay for what was not done. If I have a word for you and I do not give you the word and the word would have kept you from sinning, I am to blame for the consequences you incur. If I give you the word and you receive the word of the Lord, then the Lord will require of you whether you act on it or not. Do you understand how this reflects on us and how we are responsible for the outcome of things on earth? Noah condemned the world because of his faith in the word God spoke to him and his action as he proceeded to build an ark; meaning he was preparing for the word of God to come to pass.

It was up to Noah to receive the word of the Lord, then apply the action necessary to obey the Lord. God spoke to Noah to build an ark so his family would be saved, and the rest of the world condemned. Hebrews states, "Noah condemned the world." We know God spoke the word to condemn the world and Noah obeyed the word and the world was condemned. What mighty power we hold in us; that is, faith in God and His word! By faith, Noah changed the outcome of the natural world as he built the ark, obeying the word of the Lord.

"Faith," like "love," is an action word. Not only did Noah

believe the word of the Lord; he agreed with the word and said so by his action of building the ark. As we see in the book of James, "Faith without works is dead."

> What does it profit, my brethren, if someone says he has faith but does not have works? Can faith save him? If a brother or sister is naked and destitute of daily food, and one of you says to them, "Depart in peace, be warmed and filled," but you do not give them the things which are needed for the body, what does it profit? Thus also faith by itself, if it does not have works, is dead. But someone will say, "You have faith, and I have works." Show me your faith without your works, and I will show you my faith by my works. You believe that there is one God. You do well. Even the demons believe—and tremble! But do you want to know, O foolish man, that faith without works is dead? Was not Abraham our father justified by works when he offered Isaac his son on the altar? Do you see that faith was working together with his works, and by works faith was made perfect? And the Scripture was fulfilled which says, "Abraham believed God, and it was accounted to him for righteousness." And he was called the friend of God. You see then that a man is justified by works, and not by faith only. Likewise, was not Rahab the harlot also justified by works when she received the messengers and sent them out another way? For as the body without the spirit is dead, so faith without works is dead also."
>
> James 2:14-26

Please understand, when the Word is speaking of works, it is not saying that your works will save you, it is saying that true faith is not only words; true faith is accompanied by works. Abraham's faith was shown by his journey to sacrifice his son, his promise from God, at God's request. Abraham knew the promise was not only words, but his son, Isaac. The promise of God, that is God's word, was manifested as Isaac. The promise of God would not be killed. Abraham believed the promise would live; even as he walked up the mountain with Isaac as the sacrifice. His faith manifested in action. Abraham did not just sit in his tent and cry because God told him to sacrifice his son, God's promise to him. No! Abraham believed and by his actions, that is his faith, he showed God he believed the word of God, from the beginning.

Abraham and Noah, neither one, looked at what they saw, but looked at and received the spoken word of God by faith. This thought will propel us into a new dimension of faith and the action that brings forth the life of God's spoken word! Yes, there is life in the word of God, whether it is the written word, the "logos," or the spoken word of God, the "rhema." His breath is in all His Word. "All Scripture is given by inspiration of God, and is profitable for doctrine, for reproof, for correction, for instruction in righteousness, that the man of God may be complete, thoroughly equipped for every good work" (2 Timothy 3:16-17).

The word "inspiration" is the Greek word *theopneustos* (*the-o'-pnyü-stos*), meaning "inspired by God," (*Theos*, "God," *pneo*, "to breathe"). The root of this word means, "divinely breathed in."[21] Whenever God speaks, be it through the Bible or His

---

21   Strong's Concordance

audible voice, a dream, a vision, etc., however He speaks, know this: His very breath is upon you.

How are we to bring forth our faith into action? How do we know our faith is producing a change in this realm? We are in this realm, but not "of" this realm. In other words, we are from a different kingdom the moment we receive Jesus Christ as our Lord and Savior. We now have authority over things in this realm. Now everything has changed! We must be reminded who we are and how we operate from the spiritual realm, affecting the natural world around us. That is what Noah, Abraham, and all the testimonies of faith reveal when we study these great men and women of the Word. There are many men and women not mentioned in Hebrews 11 whose circumstances were changed by their faith, too. There are not enough volumes to write every miracle and change in this world brought forth by faith.

We must understand the concept of the Kingdom of God and its effect in this realm. Many times, because we do not have full revelation of a situation, we try to make it fit with what we think should be, instead of what God says it should be. For instance, when Peter was in the garden with Christ, on the night of His betrayal, Peter wanted to fight in the natural realm.

> When Jesus had spoken these words, He went out with His disciples over the Brook Kidron, where there was a garden, which He and His disciples entered. And Judas, who betrayed Him, also knew the place; for Jesus often met there with His disciples. Then Judas, having received a detachment of troops, and officers from the chief priests and Pharisees, came there with lanterns, torches, and weapons. Je-

sus therefore, knowing all things that would come upon Him, went forward and said to them, "Whom are you seeking?" They answered Him, "Jesus of Nazareth." Jesus said to them, "I am He." And Judas, who betrayed Him, also stood with them. Now when He said to them, "I am He," they drew back and fell to the ground. Then He asked them again, "Whom are you seeking?" And they said, "Jesus of Nazareth." (8) Jesus answered, "I have told you that I am He. Therefore, if you seek Me, let these go their way," that the saying might be fulfilled which He spoke, "Of those whom You gave Me I have lost none." Then Simon Peter, having a sword, drew it and struck the high priest's servant, and cut off his right ear. The servant's name was Malchus. So Jesus said to Peter, "Put your sword into the sheath. Shall I not drink the cup which My Father has given Me?"

John 18:1-11

Peter did not understand nor comprehend; that is, he did not have the revelation of what was truly happening in the garden. Peter wanted to fight in the natural realm and defeat the Roman soldiers, proving he would fight for Jesus to the death, as he stated in Luke.

> And the Lord said, "Simon, Simon! Indeed, Satan has asked for you, that he may sift you as wheat. But I have prayed for you, that your faith should not fail; and when you have returned to Me, strengthen your brethren." But he said to Him, "Lord, I am ready to go with You, both to prison and to death." Then

> He said, "I tell you, Peter, the rooster shall not crow this day before you will deny three times that you know Me."
>
> Luke 22:31-34

Peter was prepared to fight the natural battle, because he was unaware of the true reason Jesus came. Jesus was not here to overthrow the Roman government. Jesus came to overthrow all kingdoms set up by man. The only way to do that was to die on the Cross and rise again, ascending to the right hand of Father with all authority in His hands. That is why he told Peter: "Put your sword into the sheath. Shall I not drink the cup which My Father has given Me?" (John 18:11). Peter had a sword in his hand, prepared to battle in the garden with Christ. When the Soldiers came to take Christ away, Peter pulled a sword to fight.

> When those around Him saw what was going to happen, they said to Him, "Lord, shall we strike with the sword?" And one of them struck the servant of the high priest and cut off his right ear. But Jesus answered and said, "Permit even this." And He touched his ear and healed him.
>
> Luke 22:49-51

Peter was thinking only of what he could do to stand by Christ in the natural realm, he was not fully aware of God's perfect plan for Humanity. It was not just about Peter and that moment, it was about something bigger than Peter. Peter and the disciples believed Jesus was going to deliver them from the tyranny of the Roman occupation and in His own way, Jesus did accomplish that; but the disciples could not look past their situation into the realm of the spirit to see God's perspective for the world. Their eyes and ears were not open to the realm of God, only to what they saw right in front of them. Our eyes must look past where we are in the temporal world and see where we are in the heavenly world of Christ.

Malchus was the servant of the high priest according to the Book of John: "Then Simon Peter, having a sword, drew it and struck the high priest's servant, and cut off his right ear. The servant's name was Malchus" (John 18:10).

This incident was a prophetic view of things to come. The name "Malchus" in Greek means "king or kingdom." Malchus was the servant of the high priest and Peter cut off his right ear. Malchus represents the servant of the high priest of this world, while Christ is the High Priest over all the world and all kingdoms. Malchus was a form of a servant representing this world. Peter wanted to destroy the natural kingdom, while Christ was setting up His eternal Kingdom.

Malchus' right ear was cut off, meaning he had lost his hearing. "Faith comes by hearing and hearing the word of God" (Romans 10:17).

The hearing of the world is in trouble. Some choose not to hear the truth. Even so, God is opening up ears to hear the truth through His Holy Spirit and the servants (us) of the Most High Priest, Ruler over all things! Speak those things that are not as though they were.

Our actions, by faith, reflect what God has spoken in the spiritual realm. We hear the Word, we have faith in God, and we act on what He has spoken. Change comes by faith. Moving and shaking this world with our faith in Him and our words spoken, either in prayers, decrees, declarations, or proclamations! Agree with God and see the fire of the Holy One fall from the heavens and burn the unholy out of our lives. God is a consuming fire; may He consume you fully!

Chapter Ten

In 2012 I went through a tough time, I was diagnosed with breast cancer. God has told me to share, and I want people to understand what it is like when the miracle you are believing for does not happen the way you want it to happen. Let me say first, I do not understand all of God's ways. I do have a relationship with my Jesus, Holy Spirit, and Father, that I believe is intimate and close. He tells me all the time how much He loves me, and His love overflows so much at times, I cannot speak or relay what has occurred between us.

In October of 2011, I was preparing for my yearly mammogram and inside I felt "off." Something was not right. I expected something to show on the mammogram, so when it came back clear I was surprised. I asked the Lord if I had missed it. Had I not heard Holy Spirit correctly? Two weeks later, during a routine breast exam discharge came out of my right breast. I was like, "Guess I did hear You clearly, Lord." I knew something was wrong. I prayed and sought the Lord for what to do. At the time, my husband was preparing for major surgery and I did not want to tell him until after his surgery. I wanted him to get through his surgery and recovery without this on his mind. So, I called the doctor to have this checked out. But I went numerous times and no discharge would come out. Unless the discharge came out the doctor could not diagnose what the discharge was. I finally told my husband what was happening with me and by now it was early spring of the following year, 2012.

During worship one Sunday, the Holy Spirit spoke to me and said, "This is not unto death." Praise the Lord! Just like Gideon, the Lord knew exactly what I needed to hear to increase my faith to walk with Him through this journey. I did not know what lay ahead, but I do know what did not lay ahead, and that was death from this invasion. Hallelujah! I am a prophetess, a prophet of the Lord, and I hear for myself and others. I trust Him no matter the situation. I have seen healings, deliverances, salvations, and much more. I expected my healing by the power of the Holy Spirit—a miracle. I read the Scriptures, especially the ones regarding healing. I spoke and believed for my miracle. I could not wait to go the doctors and have them retest everything so they could tell me—there is nothing there! That was not what happened.

As the doctor visits increased and the diagnosis was breast cancer, with the prognosis of a mastectomy, I stood believing the Lord for His supernatural healing. This went on from the middle of April to June. I did not hear the Lord say, "I will heal you and you will not have to walk through this." What I heard continually was, "I AM with you." Thank You Lord!

There were many times when the Lord was with me and taking care of me. He continued to speak to me and was with me in many of my needs. I would just speak something like, "Lord, I need a magazine rack." I went to work not long after that and there was my magazine rack with a sign on it, "Free." That was mine! Praise God! Another time I was telling the Lord, "I need check registers and if I don't find any (which I did not), I will go the bank and pick some up after the surgery." Well, once again my Father came though and my husband was cleaning out his desk area and asked me if I needed any of "these." These what? Check registers! He had a handful of them for me! And then, another time I told the Lord, "I need some new house shoes before I go into the hospital for the surgery." Again, my Jesus is too good to me! I went to work one day, not along before the surgery and a friend gave me a brand-new pair of house shoes, just my size! All this says how much my God cares about every little thing in my life, every little thing! I spoke and He gave me just what I needed.

There was a night, though, when I awoke and wept before the Lord, still expecting my supernatural healing. My Father and I spent the night on the living room floor in conversation about all that was happening. I prayed and I cried. I wept and I prayed. He loved me and hugged me. Father was so very near me during my time of weeping and questioning Him. God then spoke to me, "Are you finished, Brenda?" I said, "Yes, Lord." I was tired and weary from the tears and the prayers for my healing. I sat up and moved to my chair and rested. The Lord said, "Good! Are you ready to walk with Me through this?" I answered Him, "Yes," and I complained one more time about the scars and my body and how I would look. My sweet Father answered me with this, "Brenda, My Son has scars." And I wept all the more. We loved on one another and I pulled my big girl panties up and spoke to Him, "I am ready to walk with You wherever You go. As long as You are with me, I am good."

There is so much more to this testimony, this is the short version, but apparently, I was to share it for someone reading this. I do not claim to know all and understand all. I do know that my Father in heaven loves me more than I love myself and He, He alone, knows what I need to move on in this world. I will say this, after all is said and done; I would not change the time I spent with my Father in intimacy and closeness during this season for anything in this world. I would go through it again just to be near Him.

My faith is not just about "get me out of this situation." My faith is about walking with my Father in all aspects of my life. I am not angry with Him because I have to bear something I did not want to bear. I am not disappointed in Him because He did not heal me the way I wanted Him to heal me. The miracle of healing did not come, and I could have chosen to be bitter and angry, walking away from God. Many abandon God when they "go through." I am closer with Him and know Him at a level I never would have known Him if I had not walked this with Him. And yes, I walked with Him, as Gideon, too, decided to walk with Father God in a time of uncertainty; a time of not knowing what was happening until it became clear. Gideon understood the love of God and his faith was increased because he knew God was there with him, no matter the task. I understand that now, and I am blessed and highly favored of the Lord as my faith has increased in times of uncertainty. I know that I know that I know God will never leave me nor forsake me! He has proven it time and time again.

Paul states that trials and tribulations bring patience and perseverance. (See Romans 5:3; Ephesians 3:13; 2 Thessalonians 1:4.) We are not to despise what we go though. Our faith increases and our relationship with Father becomes more intimate during times of uncertainty. When you walk closely with someone in this world, you are there with them and for them, no matter what is happening. God is like that with us, He does not leave us just because the journey has a few bumps in the road. I will run the race, no matter how many times I stumble or fall, I will be victorious walking with Him.

Chapter Eleven

Now faith is…

We continually listen to sermons and messages in the body of Christ about how little our faith may be in any given circumstance. I am here to remind you how great your faith can and will be in Christ! Faith is not about faith in you, nor faith in money, nor faith in man. Faith is all about God! What does He say and how does He accomplish what He states in His word? God uses us, His beautiful creation, to complete His will on earth as it is in heaven.

Faith sees and hears beyond the natural realm, into the realm of God, His place of dwelling; that is, heaven. How can we reach into the realm where God's word is always manifested to His perfect will? There are many Scriptures that speak of faith There are two places in Scripture when Christ speaks of "great faith." In this chapter we will discuss the first Scripture:

> Now when Jesus had entered Capernaum, a centurion came to Him, pleading with Him saying, "Lord, my servant is lying at home paralyzed, dreadfully tormented." And Jesus said to him, "I will come and heal him." The centurion answered and said, "Lord, I am not worthy that You should come under my roof. But only speak a word, and my servant will be healed. For I also am a man under authority, having soldiers under me. And I say to this one, 'Go,' and he goes; and to another, 'Come,' and he comes; and to my servant, 'Do this,' and he does it.'" When

Jesus heard it, He marveled, and said to those who followed, "Assuredly, I say to you, I have not found such **great faith**, not even in Israel! And I say to you that many will come from east and west, and sit down with Abraham, Isaac, and Jacob in the kingdom of heaven. But the sons of the kingdom will be cast out into outer darkness. There will be weeping and gnashing of teeth." Then Jesus said to the centurion, "Go your way; and as you have believed, so let it be done for you." And his servant was healed that same hour.

Matthew 8:5-13

Let us look at the many things going on in this Scripture, so we may fully understand what is happening and why Christ was so amazed at this man's faith. First, we have a centurion, a Roman, a Gentile—he was not Jewish. The Romans were hated by the Jewish people; they had conquered them, and they controlled them through oppression. Jesus was the Messiah of the Jewish people, according to His own words, "I was not sent except to the lost sheep of the house of Israel" (Matthew 15:24).

Many of the Jewish people believed that Christ was their Messiah, the One who would free them from the oppressing hand of Rome. Christ was and is the Messiah of the Jewish people, as well as the Messiah of the entire world. The Jewish people believed that He would come into Jerusalem and defeat the Roman stronghold, and Christ would be crowned king in the natural realm. That was not God's plan. Christ came to save the world. "For God so loved the world, that He gave His only begotten Son, that whoever believes in Him should not perish but have everlasting life" (John 3:16).

Did the centurion, an officer in the Roman army, understand he was not received by the others hanging around with Christ? I am sure he was fully aware of his place in this society. He had to know he was hated by the Jewish people. The centurion was not welcomed by the people, more than likely he was feared by them, and rightfully so. Yet, that did not stop this Roman officer from approaching Christ and asking for something from Him, in front of all those gathered around Christ. He needed something from Him, the healing he was asking for was not for himself, it was for his servant, who was at home dying.

"So when **he heard about Jesus**, he sent elders of the Jews to Him, pleading with Him to come and heal his servant" (Luke 7:3). This man "heard" of Jesus. This centurion heard of the healings, the miracles, the signs, and the wonders performed by this man of Jewish descent and he sought Him out to receive from Him what belonged to the Jews. For this man, it was not about his place in society, it was about the healing his servant needed. He was not afraid to approach Christ, in front of everyone, and ask Him for something.

Apparently, this man knew who he was, and who Christ was; for as he asked for the healing of his servant, he also told Christ he was not worthy for Christ to come to his home. He tells Christ, "All You have to do is speak a word and my servant will be healed."

In this Scripture, the Roman centurion understands authority, natural authority. "I say to this one, 'Come and he comes,' and this one, 'Go and he goes.'" The centurion recognizes the authority of Christ, that is why he tells Him, "Only speak a word, and my servant will be healed," in verse eight.

Christ walks in an authority that is not only natural, but in the spiritual authority of the heavenly realm, and this centurion understood this kingdom concept of authority. Earlier I spoke of the authority we have in Christ, and in this Scripture, it is spoken of by Christ Himself.

Kingdom authority is not given to only a few, but to all who come to Christ. It is important to understand authority, kingdom authority. Just as the centurion spoke to Christ, "You do not even have to come to my home, just speak and it will be done." My God, that is faith! And this kind of faith, great faith, understands kingdom authority. Knowing your authority in Christ is the key to the great faith mentioned in this scripture.

The great faith the centurion showed was based upon his understanding of natural authority and implementing this same concept into the realm of the Spirit. When the centurion gave an order to others; he spoke and expected his order to be followed. He did not expect to have to go check and see if the order had been carried out. When he spoke, he knew what he spoke would be taken care of by those under him. He understood something about authority; you did not need to be there to be sure the task was complete, because he knew his will and order would manifest.

The centurion transferred this concept from this realm to the spiritual realm. He was saying to Christ, "All You have to do is speak and it will be completed, whatever You say, because I recognize that You carry authority, and I understand authority." Authority is not limited to time and space. In other words, when I speak into the heavenly realm, I do not have to see the completion of my words right then, I know by faith, that what I requested is already complete in heaven, because I am in alignment with the will of God!

The centurion knew he was in alignment with those who were over him when he gave an order. The same concept applies in the spirit realm. When I am in alignment with the will of God, I know it will be done on earth as it is in heaven; therefore, I am bringing His will from heaven, where His word is already settled, and it is manifested before my eyes. The centurion's faith went beyond space. He believed that Christ did not have to be where his sick servant was (in the natural) because the authority of Christ flows past space. The buildings men build cannot stop the faith we have in God. Holy Spirit is not hindered by time nor space when great faith is exercised. The centurion understood natural authority and transferred that same principal into the spirit realm to receive what he requested!

Authority is something you exercise, like your faith. You must realize you have the authority to utilize the power Christ has given to you in His death, burial, resurrection, and ascension to heaven. He is now sitting at the right hand of Father! That is where you sit, next to God. Christ is in you and you are in Him. According to John 17, we are one with the Father, Son, and Holy Spirit! The same power that raised Christ from the dead is in you! You must believe and receive from Christ all He has given.

Authority is the right to use the power you have. The enemy has power, but as we discussed earlier, it has been made null and void by the cross in the body of Christ! The authority given to Satan by the first man, Adam, was taken back at the cross, by our Lord and Savior, Jesus! Christ returned our authority back to us when He opened the heavens by His death; that is, when the veil was torn from top to bottom and the heavens were once again opened and now you carry the authority of God wherever you walk! Most of the body is not aware they have any authority at all. Here is my next question: "Are you utilizing your authority to complete God's perfect will on earth as it is in heaven, not just for you, but for the body as a whole?"

"For the word of God is living and powerful, and sharper than any two-edged sword, piercing even to the division of soul and spirit, and of joints and marrow, and is a discerner of the thoughts and intents of the heart" (Hebrews 4:12). The word of God, Christ Himself, is powerful; but if you never speak the Word or understand the power He is, you are not walking in your authority. We must know who we are in Him. When I speak of "knowing," I am talking about "experiencing" Christ in every way. Not just knowing of Him, but truly experiencing His name (His character, His heart). The authority God has given you is the ability to access all He is and transform the world in His love.

The centurion's response is what caused Christ to use the term, "great faith." The centurion understood authority, and yet, he saw what many of Christ's disciples could not see; that is, Christ is here for all of us. I, too, can receive from Him and partake of His realm. As we read in Matthew, Christ adds to His response to the centurion: "And I say to you that many will come from east and west, and sit down with Abraham, Isaac, and Jacob in the kingdom of heaven. But the sons of the kingdom will be cast out into outer darkness. There will be weeping and gnashing of teeth." (Matthew 8:11-12).

Christ is talking about the Jewish people and the Gentiles in this Scripture. He is very clear in His response to the centurion. "I came for certain ones, and not all of them will sit with Me; therefore, I receive those who receive Me." In other words, "I will include the Gentiles, even though the ones I came for do not understand this. I have come for the entire world, not just a few." When Peter is called to the Gentiles, he is given a vision.

> The next day, as they went on their journey and drew near the city, Peter went up on the housetop to pray, about the sixth hour. Then he became very hungry and wanted to eat; but while they made ready, he fell into a trance and saw heaven opened and an object like a great sheet bound at the four corners, descending to him and let down to the earth. In it were all kinds of four-footed animals of the earth, wild beasts, creeping things, and birds of the air. And a voice came to him, "Rise, Peter; kill and eat." But Peter said, "Not so, Lord! For I have never eaten anything common or unclean." And a voice spoke to him again the second time, "What God has cleansed you must not call common." This was done three times. And the object was taken up into heaven again.
>
> Acts 10:9-16

Peter does not immediately understand what God is saying in the vision, and as he inquires of the Lord, Holy Spirit speaks to him and gives Peter guidance. (See Acts 10:19-20.)

> Then he said to them, "You know how unlawful it is for a Jewish man to keep company with or go to one of another nation. But God has shown me that I should not call any man common or unclean." Then Peter opened his mouthed said, "In truth I perceive

God shows no partiality, but in every nation whoever heard Him and works righteousness is accepted by Him."

Acts 10:28,34

Peter received the revelation of the vision and he accepted what God spoke; Christ came for the Gentiles, too. The revelation of this truth was not given to Peter until after the death of Christ, and yet, Christ mentions this concept to the centurion. Why? Because the "great faith" of the Roman centurion went beyond the natural realm; the natural thought of how things are in the eyes of people! This man stopped the religious spirit in its tracks and released Holy Spirit to move through Christ for his miracle! By his faith (which was revealed by his words), this man went past the time and space of that day and moved into the future, into a time when the Gentiles would receive Christ by His grace and love for us all.

The authority of Christ is not limited to a select few, it given to all who receive Christ as their Lord and Savior and to all those who believe and have faith in God. Look past where you are and into the future by faith. Look past where you are in this realm of earthly things and move yourself, by your faith in God, into the realm of the spirit, bringing forth heaven on earth. What is heaven? It is the place where God dwells. His word is not complicated in heaven. His word is not attacked in heaven. His word is not void of power in heaven. His word goes forth and accomplishes what He sends it to do in heaven. Heaven on earth is not just a saying that sounds good and keeps us pacified until the day Christ returns. No! Heaven on earth is possible through our faith in God and God alone.

The Body (that is you and me) has the authority to bring

heaven on earth through our faith in God, by looking past anything in this realm that is stopping our view. For instance, if you look past the natural realm and gaze into the heavenly realm of God, you can see past the hindrances and into the will of God, just for you. Believe the Word of God; that is, Christ. Believe that heaven is now open to you and you can see into the realm of God by faith!

In heaven there is constant worship. The glory of God is always in His fullness. The power of Holy Spirit is not quenched. Our Savior, Jesus Christ, sits at the right hand of Father and speaks on our behalf. There are colors in heaven never seen in this realm. The sound of worship is a sound not familiar here on earth, it is a different sound, for the angels worship Him around His throne continually! Continual worship. My God, can you image His Presence? His glory? The beauty of the One Who was, and is, and is to come? The power and sound of His voice? There is much more to Heaven than what we can imagine. I want Him on earth as He is in heaven, in His home! I am His resting place and home here on earth.

Chapter Twelve

As we learned in the previous chapter, there are kingdom principles we can apply to our lives on earth and they will manifest God's will. The centurion recognized authority and because he was familiar with how it worked on earth, he related that same principle to the spirit realm. God's principles can manifest here as we see in the Scriptures: Kingdom Authority, Kingdom Grace, and Kingdom Humility. The Kingdom of God is your option to walk in, when you are a child of God. It is time for the body of Christ to stop looking at other options and depend solely upon our Lord and Savior Jesus Christ!

The second example in the Scriptures that speaks of great faith, is a woman whose daughter was demon possessed. She had encounter with Christ. The scriptures about this woman are short and to the point.

> Then Jesus went out from there and departed to the region of Tyre and Sidon. And behold, a woman of Canaan came from that region and cried out to Him, saying, "Have mercy on me, O Lord, Son of David! My daughter is severely demon-possessed." But He answered her not a word. And His disciples came and urged Him, saying, "Send her away, for she cries out after us." But He answered and said, "I was not sent except to the lost sheep of the house of Israel." Then she came and worshiped Him, saying, "Lord, help me!" But He answered and said, "It is not good to take the children's bread and throw it

to the little dogs." And she said, "Yes, Lord, yet even the little dogs eat the crumbs which fall from their masters' table." Then Jesus answered and said to her, "O woman, great is your faith! Let it be to you as you desire." And her daughter was healed from that very hour.

Matthew 15:21-28

From there He arose and went to the region of Tyre and Sidon. And He entered a house and wanted no one to know it, but He could not be hidden. For a woman whose young daughter had an unclean spirit heard about Him, and she came and fell at His feet. The woman was a Greek, a Syro-Phoenician by birth, and she kept asking Him to cast the demon out of her daughter. But Jesus said to her, "Let the children be filled first, for it is not good to take the children's bread and throw it to the little dogs." And she answered and said to Him, "Yes, Lord, yet even the little dogs under the table eat from the children's crumbs." Then He said to her, "For this saying go your way; the demon has gone out of your daughter." And when she had come to her house, she found the demon gone out, and her daughter lying on the bed.

Mark 7:24-30

You have heard me throughout this book speak about how I love this person or I am amazed by this one's faith. This woman makes me shout, "GLORY!!!" Faith is not just words spoken, faith is moving into the spiritual realm along with your words.

In this scripture, Jesus is headed to Tyre and Sidon. This is the same area Elijah had gone to in 1 Kings17. During the time Elijah visited a woman and her son, there was a famine in the land, and yet, they had plenty of food during this time. The prophet being with them brought blessings to their household. This famine was a result of the word Elijah prophesied to King Ahab in 1 Kings 17:1. This area, Zarephath, was also in Sidon, where none other than Jezebel originated, she was Phoenician as well. This area was mostly pagan and the demonic was allowed to prosper. I find it interesting, this woman, from Canaan, had no problem approaching Jesus. She was bold. "And behold, a woman of Canaan came from that region and cried out to Him saying, 'Have mercy upon me, O Lord, Son of David! My daughter is serenely demon-possessed.'" (Matthew 15:22).

When this woman "cried out," she was not just crying; she was making a clamor, she was shouting or screaming. She was prepared to make a fool of herself, in the eyes of those present, to receive her miracle. She was not trying to come in the appropriate manner of the culture of that day. No! This woman was making a scene and did not care who heard her or what they thought of her. Is it possible when we need a miracle from God, we are more concerned what others around us may think?

I am not going to dwell on the history of this area in this book. That is not my intention. But I want you to understand the area she was from and how she was raised. We know she boldly approached the Messiah and immediately addressed Him as "Lord, Son of David." Stop right there. She addressed Jesus with a title that was used only by the Jews. She is not Jewish! She was trying to come to Him as one of His culture and nation. She was presenting herself as someone she was not, a woman of Jewish heritage. She was wearing a mask, hiding her true identity in hopes of receiving from Him what she needed. I am sure she hoped Christ would not realize who she really was, a Gentile.

I cannot say what was going through her mind, but I can put myself in her situation. I know I would do whatever was necessary to get the miracle I needed for my child. I would have no problem addressing Jesus with the title of "Son of David." Did she know what she was saying? I believe she did. This woman was ignored by Jesus. She was not prepared to be ignored. Jesus answered her not a word.

Why should He respond to her? This woman was not being honest with Christ; she was trying to hide who she was and where she was from. When you come to Jesus do not think for one second you can come hiding things about yourself, He knows all. When you come before Him, He has already seen you, just as you are. No mask, no deceit, no lies and He accepts you just as you are!

In this story, the disciples want her to leave. The disciples do not want her around Christ, she was a Gentile and they knew it. Jesus replies to her, telling her He is only sent for the house of Israel; that is, the Jewish people. In other words, He is saying, "I am not sent for you, only the Hebrew people, the House of Israel." He knew she was not of Jewish heritage. He was saying to her, "I know who you are and I am here only for certain people and you are not one of them." Okay, now how many of you would have stopped right there and said, "Oh, okay. You are not here for me. Hmmm, then I will go home." I am just saying, many of us would have walked away from Christ, without an answer to our cry or to our prayer, not this lady! She persisted to get what she needed.

This woman's response to His rebuke was worship! What? This woman did not receive the answer she was longing for, and yet, she stayed and fell at the feet of the Savior! She no longer tried to masquerade herself as a Jew. This mother was desperate. Can you imagine her thoughts? I am not leaving here until I get my daughter healed. I will persevere. I will press-in. I will not take "no" for an answer. I have been everywhere, to every physician and they cannot help my daughter. But I have heard about this Man, Jesus. I understand He can do what no other can do and now I am coming to Him just as I am. I am removing my mask and I will address Him accordingly, "Lord, please help me!" She lay at His feet and cried out to Him even more, only this time she was revealing exactly who she was, a Gentile. She was saying to Him, "I am not Jewish, but still I want something from you, help me! Please help me!"

This woman fell at His feet and worshipped Christ; still He denied her and adding to His denial, Jesus insulted her. He called her a dog when He told her He would not take the children's bread, that is the Children of Israel's part, and throw it to a dog. "Dog" in the Greek in this verse is kynarion (kü-nä'-rē-on), meaning a "little puppy" (more like a pet) in comparison the Greek word, kuon (we get canis from this root) means more of a hound or a mongrel (wild dog).[22] It was typical for Jewish people to use this term as an insult, meaning the ones they were addressing were ceremonially unclean, they could not enter into the New Jerusalem. Well, now how many would leave Jesus, offended?

We can be offended so easily in today's society, it has become nonsensical, just pure nonsense. What if this woman would have reacted like we believe we have a "right" to react?

---

22 Strong's Concordance

The man of God who trained me for 14 years as a Prophetess was Prophet Ronnie Moore and he used to say, "When you are in Christ, you have given up the right to be right." Hmmmm, that will make you stop, right there! Holy Spirit reminds me of this statement often. Too many times offense will keep us from our miracle. We put self first, not Christ. It is as though we have something to protect or defend. News Flash!!! God can defend Himself and Protect Himself! He is not concerned about His reputation, nor our reputation.

This woman was prepared to do whatever she had to do to get the miracle she needed for her daughter. Nothing was going to stand in her way. No one telling her "no," for her miracle. No one insulting her will stop her. She purposed in her heart, I came for something from You Jesus and I will persist until I receive it. So where does she go from here? She has positioned herself without a mask upon her face. She is coming to Him just as she is. She is worshipping Him the only way she knows. She is in need and He is the only One who has what she needs, her miracle, this is where she steps into a realm of faith very few have pressed into and experienced. Christ called her a pet, a dog. She says in her heart, Yes that is true, but, "even the little dogs eat the crumbs which fall from their masters table" (Matthew 15:27).

Wow!! What??? God, You can remind me that I am not being honest with You. You can tell me I am not in the chosen group. You can call me a dog. You can say all this, and I am going to look past where we are and jump into a place of faith I have never been before. I am here to say, "Yes I am a dog, but even I will eat what the master drops from the table. I will take and eat what fell on the floor. I will take just the little because it is enough! It is more than enough!" Christ responded with this, "O woman, great is your faith! Let it be to you as you desire" (Matthew 15:28).

How did this woman get to this place? She looked past herself. Finally, she lay before the Lord Jesus, completely naked and undone. She had no other natural way to get what she wanted, and even against opposition, she pressed in to get to the place where she was going to receive her miracle. She jumped into the spirit realm and looked past her situation and into the future with her response. She went beyond what she saw and spoke something that only God and Jesus knew; that is, when Jesus died He would die for us all, not just a select few. The heavens were open for her to see into the future by the words she spoke. The truth is, when you drop a crumb from the table (of provision) the dog will lick that crumb up, eat it and enjoy what little they received. That is a natural truth this woman took into the spirit realm. I am prepared to take whatever you give me, no matter how small. In all honesty, this was not a small thing. She received the revelation of Who Christ truly was! "Then He said to her, 'For this saying go your way; the demon has gone out of your daughter" (Mark 7:29).

Did you see His response? For this saying? "For the words in your response I am moving on your behalf! You have positioned yourself in another realm. By faith, you have moved past seeing the natural and moved into the prophetic future of the world!" She spoke out something she may not have even understood. It did not matter, she received because of her faith!

Christ told her, "I did not come except for Israel," and we know He came for us all. How far will she press in, is that what He was wondering? Will she take herself past the natural and into the spirit where all things are possible? Christ walked in open heavens. When Joshua walked with the ark into the Jordan River, the Jordan opened for him and he crossed the river. When Elijah used his mantle upon the Jordan River it opened for him. And when Elisha did the same as his father, Elijah, the River Jordan opened as well. We see when Christ came to the Jordan, He was not there to cross the river; He was there to be baptized by His cousin, John. When John baptized Jesus the Jordan did not open, but the heavens did open. The heavens are open for you and for me!

> When He had been baptized, Jesus came up immediately from the water; and behold, the heavens were opened to Him, and He saw the Spirit of God descending like a dove and alighting upon Him. And suddenly a voice came from heaven, saying, "This is My beloved Son, in whom I am well pleased."
> Matthew 3:16-17

The heavens were opened to Christ as He prepared for ministry. When Christ died on the cross and gave His last breath, according to numerous scriptures, the veil was torn in two; the veil that was between God and man, separating us from Him in the Holy of Holies. According to the scriptures in Exodus, the veil on this earth is a pattern of the veil in the heavenlies

"Then, behold, the veil of the temple was torn in two from top to bottom; and the earth quaked, and the rocks were split" (Matthew 27:51).

"Then the veil of the temple was torn in two from top to bottom" (Mark 15:38).

"Then the sun was darkened, and the veil of the temple was torn in two" (Luke 23:45).

Jesus Christ walked in open heavens during His ministry on earth. Now we are to do the same. We are able to walk in the Kingdom of Heaven. Christ continually told us the Kingdom of Heaven is near and it is at hand. He was in His Father's Kingdom, and He wanted us to be aware that we too can walk in the same place He did, under an open heaven. When the veil was torn it was torn from top to bottom, opening the dwelling place of God to us. We have access to Him, without restraint.

The woman in Matthew 15 took full advantage of the open heaven around Christ; by faith she saw and knew what others did not. When you are walking in God's open heaven, all things that He chooses to reveal can be seen. This place of God's seat is the place where thunder and lightning are produced. This is the place of the beginning of time and space and all things we know as the earthly realm. Both the visible and the invisible things are seen! She saw and she spoke what no one else could see, not even the disciples with Christ. That is why Jesus said to her, "O woman great is your faith." Her faith went past time and space as she looked into the eyes of Jesus Christ! She saw past the natural and into a place distant from the natural. She saw the spirit realm where there is no time nor space; the place eternity dwells, opening everything up to our very eyes!

> Therefore he sent horses and chariots and a great army there, and they came by night and surrounded the city. And when the servant of the man of God arose early and went out, there was an army, surrounding the city with horses and chariots. And his servant said to him, "Alas, my master! What shall we do?" So he answered, "Do not fear, for those who

are with us are more than those who are with them." And Elisha prayed, and said, "Lord, I pray, open his eyes that he may see." Then the Lord opened the eyes of the young man, and he saw. And behold, the mountain was full of horses and chariots of fire all around Elisha."

2 Kings 6:14-17

This is a perfect example of how the Lord can show you something no one else may see, when you are desperate and seeking Him for answers. Elisha asked God to open the eyes of his servant so he could see what Elisha already saw in the spirit. Just because you do not see it, does not mean it is not there; it just has not been revealed to you. The Spirit realm is real, and it is filled with activity all around you. This woman of faith saw into the Spirit realm. She saw the future when the Gentiles would receive what the Jewish people did not want from Christ.

Take your eyes off the natural realm and seek Holy Spirit for God's will in your life; ask Him to reveal what He already knows. Look past the obstacles and into the heavens for God's best for you! What are you seeking form God? Ask Him to show it to you in His realm.

Chapter Thirteen

The Roman centurion and the woman with the demon-possessed daughter had similar circumstances in their lives, and when they met Christ, they found their lives were never the same. Let us look at the similarities of these two Gentiles who boldly came to the Grace of God that is Christ!

The centurion walked in Kingdom Authority; while the woman walked in Kingdom Grace and Mercy. They both received what they saw; even though they walked different paths there were similar patterns between them. There were five similarities that jumped out at me as I read and studied these amazing people.

1. Both Had No Other Option
2. Both Were Gentiles
3. Both Came For Someone Else
4. Both Humbled Themselves Before Christ
5. Both Responded In Faith

Both Had No Other Option

First, they had no other option; they were desperate for what they needed. Their desperation had pushed them beyond their comfort zones, moving them to do what was necessary for the sake of one of their loved ones. It was no longer about them, neither their pride nor their reputations seemed to be important at this time. Think about it for a moment, the Roman centurion was a high-ranking officer in the army that oppressed the Jewish people. How dare he come to the Jewish Messiah and ask Him for anything after the way he had treated God's own people? Do you think that may have been the mindset of those hanging around Jesus? We know from the Samaritan woman at the well and the woman with the demon-possessed daughter, Jesus talked to the ones the society said He should not talk with in public! Both of these Gentiles had gone through every other option in their lives. I am sure, like the woman with the issue of blood, these two had seen physicians, called on their family and friends for advice, searched for every possible remedy, all to no avail. Their loved ones were still dying. They needed something no physician or family member or friend could give them—they needed a miracle. When all the doctors and the specialists give up on your condition, know this: There is a GOD Who is able to turn it all around! In all truth, it is God we should turn to at the beginning of our tribulations. Usually, though, like many in the Word, we look elsewhere, first.

"'Come now, and let us reason together,' Says the Lord, 'Though your sins are like scarlet, They shall be as white as snow; Though they are red like crimson, They shall be as wool'" (Isaiah 1:18).

"Come to Me, all you who labor and are heavy laden, and I will give you rest. Take My yoke upon you and learn from Me, for I am gentle and lowly in heart, and you will find rest for your souls. For My yoke is easy and My burden is light" (Matthew 11:27-30).

Both Were Gentiles

Secondly, these two awesome people decided they had to turn away from the god they served; and look to the One True God, Jesus Christ. The Roman centurion and the woman who approached Jesus did not serve the God we know as Jehovah. The Romans mainly worshipped their leader, such as Julius Caesar or Alexander the Great, etc. These men of Rome portrayed themselves as god and therefore they expected to be worshipped like a god. There was astrology, mysticism, sorcery, idol worship, and self-worship; much like it is in todays' culture. Judaism was the religion of the Jewish people; led by the religious leaders of the day, the High Priest, the Sadducees, and the Pharisees. These religious groups were shaken when Christ, the Son of the True God, came upon the scene. Jesus loved those who were not lovable to the society of the day, as we see through many stories in the Bible. Jesus spoke different words than the religious leaders. Christ was not about keeping rules; Christ was about loving God and others as yourself, treating all people with dignity and respect. That does not mean He accepted sin as a lifestyle, no, He loved past the sin and past the issues in people's lives. Christ embraced those whom many others ostracized. He was a different God. Jesus demonstrated a new way to see love, grace, mercy, and peace. These two Gentiles wanted access to this Man, the Man Who was fully God and fully man. They may not have understood all the "theology" but they knew they needed someone, something more than who or what they had been serving. The words of Christ say it all: "The thief does not come except to steal, and to kill, and to destroy. I have come that they may have life, and that they may have it more abundantly" (John 10:10).

Both Came For Someone Else

The centurion and the woman did not come because they were physically suffering. They came because someone they loved was suffering. The centurion had a servant who he loved, he wasn't coming so his servant could continue to serve in that regard; he came because he truly loved this man who had served him and he wanted to see him healed and see him live. There was true love and compassion in this army officer's heart for one who had served him in his life. He was suffering because someone he cared for was suffering. He experienced true compassion. Christ is the epiphany of compassion. He shows us how to live, putting others ahead of our own selfish needs and concerns.

The woman, too, was suffering, not for a servant or friend, but for her daughter. Her daughter was demon possessed, there was no arguing semantics; her daughter was suffering in a different way. It must have been torment for this woman to know her daughter was in bondage to a demon; seeing the effects of the possession had to be heart breaking. She did not come for self but for someone else. She stood in the gap for her daughter and the Centurion stood in the gap for his servant. These two stood as Christ stood for the world. Christ did not come for Himself. He came for you and me. He stood in the gap for us. He died on the cross so we would not have to die in our sin.

Christ is the One Who stood in the gap and also is the One Who's compassion overflowed from heaven to this early realm. He did not have to come to this earth and die for us, He chose to step out of eternity, out of His heavenly realm into the realm of humanity and die for you and for me. Through His death we are able to walk with Him under the open heaven!

Both Humbled Themselves Before Christ

I am not sure if ever in my lifetime (and yes, I have already stated I am over 50, actually now over 60) I have ever seen such arrogance and pride in man as I have the past 10-20 years. The Scripture tells us in Genesis that there were three temptations in the garden. "So when the woman saw that the tree was good for food, that it was pleasant to the eyes, and a tree desirable to make one wise, she took of its fruit and ate. She also gave to her husband with her, and he ate" (Genesis 3:6).

These are called, "the lust of the flesh, the lust of the eyes, and the pride of life." The fruit was "good for food," that is, the lust of the flesh; the fruit was "pleasant to the eyes," meaning the food looked good—the lust of the eyes; and lastly, the fruit would "make one wise," this reveals the pride of life that is in each and every one of us.

> Do not love the world or the things in the world. If anyone loves the world, the love of the Father is not in him. For all that is in the world—the lust of the flesh, the lust of the eyes, and the pride of life—is not of the Father but is of the world. And the world is passing away, and the lust of it; but he who does the will of God abides forever.
>
> 1 John 2:15-17

The centurion and the woman with the demon-possessed daughter both had to purpose in their hearts, they would do whatever it took to receive the miracle they needed, and reputation was no longer an issue. Remember, the centurion was an officer in the Roman army and by his own words he held authority, "I say to this one go and he goes and to this one come and he comes." He understood authority and the pride of life. I am sure he walked in pride as he oppressed those under him, as well as the Jewish people whom the Romans had conquered. It was easy for him to be prideful. And the woman, being a Syro-Phoenician in Canaan, knew she would not be received, but that did not hinder her determination. Tyre and Sidon, as I stated earlier, was the home of Jezebel and was typically considered an enemy of Israel. Remember, she came before Jesus and cried out. She shouted for Him to help her. She made a scene before all the others around Him. She was not concerned how she looked to others around the Messiah. She was only concerned for her daughter and she was prepared to do whatever it took to see her daughter free from the demon that laid hold of her. The spirit of Pride would not have allowed her to act this way in public.

Both of these people, the officer and woman, prepared to humble themselves before Jesus, no matter their place in society, and that is exactly what they did. The centurion told Jesus, I am not worthy for You to even come to my home. He recognized the authority and power in Christ and gave Jesus His due honor. This officer, who had many at his beck and call, laid down his own position, his man-given position, before Jesus and humbled himself in front of all the Jewish and Roman people present! Can you imagine what the others around him thought, especially his Roman companions?

And this woman, her people more than likely enemies of Israel, came before Christ shouting her need. I am sure as the others looked on they were perplexed as to what she was doing and why. When you come to a place in your life where there is no help, except through the One King Jesus, you realize how majestic God truly is. She humbled herself before Christ and all those present. She did not care what she looked like or how she sounded. She laid down before this Man in worship to get the answer she needed for her daughter.

We cannot come before Christ as though we deserve a thing. We must come to a place in ourselves where we know Who He is and who we are. Man has always been prideful and now we see the consequences of this pride upon our country and our world. Even in the Body of Christ, I see much pride, too much all-about-me attitude. We are the creation, while He is the Creator. We must humble ourselves and look to Christ upon our knees. Everything we say or do reveals the posture of the heart. This next Scripture says it all. "For out of the abundance of the heart the mouth speaks" (Matthew 12:34).

Both Responded in Faith

When we are in a dilemma, how we respond says everything about where we are in our walk with Christ. How do you respond when you are between a "rock and a hard place?" Do you "look to the hills where your help comes from?" Do you shake your fist at God, filled with anger because you are "going through" something? Your response to your situation makes all the difference in your walk of faith.

Please hear my heart. All of us, at some point, respond outside of faith. We respond in anger, fear, sorrow, hurt, pain, and other emotions we may not chose to share with others; and that is ok. We are all human and not one of us is without sin. Not one of us is perfect. Christ is the only One, perfect Man. It is normal to react in our human emotions and desires sometimes. And yet, once we are in Christ, we now have Another who helps us to be more like Him, Holy Spirit. Holy Spirit will help you with whatever you ask Him. Anything! It is up to us to believe Him, believe His Word, Believe He wants the best for you. This does not mean we will never "go through" anything in this world. It means, when we do "go through," we know He is with us and able to help us.

My faith is not in man, not in self, it is only in Jesus Christ, my Savior. Our faith determines our next step. I have seen many brothers and sisters leave the fellowship of one another because of offense or hurt. Some do not even go to Sunday services anymore, even after serving for 20-30 years in a local body of believers. Do not forsake the assembly of one another just because man hurt you—your faith is not in man, but in God. (See Hebrews 10:25.) It is not always easy to respond in faith, but it is always possible. You must look at the situation, seeking God for the answers, seeking Holy Spirit for help. How you respond to someone or something reveals your walk with Christ, it reveals your true heart. Do you believe God loves you? Do you believe He wants the best for you? Do you believe He can do anything?

> And when He came to the disciples, He saw a great multitude around them, and scribes disputing with them. Immediately, when they saw Him, all the people were greatly amazed, and running to Him, greeted Him. And He asked the scribes, "What are you discussing with them?" Then one of the crowd answered and said, "Teacher, I brought You my son, who has a mute spirit. And wherever it seizes him, it throws him down; he foams at the mouth, gnashes his teeth, and becomes rigid. So I spoke to Your disciples, that they should cast it out, but they could not." He answered him and said, "O faithless generation, how long shall I be with you? How long shall I bear with you? Bring him to Me." Then they brought him to Him. And when he saw Him, immediately the spirit convulsed him, and he fell on the ground and wallowed, foaming at the mouth. So He asked his father, "How long has this been happening to him?" And he said, "From childhood. And often he has thrown him both into the fire and into the water to destroy him. But if You can do anything, have compassion on us and help us." Jesus

said to him, "If you can believe, all things are possible to him who believes." Immediately the father of the child cried out and said with tears, "Lord, I believe; help my unbelief!" When Jesus saw that the people came running together, He rebuked the unclean spirit, saying to it, "Deaf and dumb spirit, I command you, come out of him and enter him no more!" Then the spirit cried out, convulsed him greatly, and came out of him. And he became as one dead, so that many said, "He is dead." But Jesus took him by the hand and lifted him up, and he arose. And when He had come into the house, His disciples asked Him privately, "Why could we not cast it out?" So He said to them, "This kind can come out by nothing but prayer and fasting."

Mark 9:14-27

This is a perfect example of how we can respond to Christ in our situation. I love this man, he is truthful to Jesus. "Yes, I believe, but help my unbelief! I can't see past my dilemma - help me to look beyond the natural world and into the world of faith in God. Help my unbelief!" We must come to Jesus completely undone, hiding nothing from Him. (He knows it all anyway.) He wants you to see you need Him. You need faith in God to be all you are in Christ! "Jesus said, 'If? There are no 'ifs' among believers. Anything can happen.' No sooner were the words out of his mouth than the father cried, 'Then I believe. Help me with my doubts!'" (Mark 9:23-24 MSG).

The reply Jesus gives this man is awesome. Jesus does not expect this man to doubt that He can do what this man has asked—IF? There are no "ifs" among the body of Christ! "If" should not even be in my vocabulary when it comes to my walk in Christ! God can do anything! If you can believe all things are possible according to Mark 9:23, stop doubting God. He is for you, not against you. If God is for you (which He is) who can be against you? Believe His promises; they are all yes and amen in Christ! "But Jesus looked at them and said, 'With men it is impossible, but not with God; for with God all things are possible'" (Mark 10:27).

It is important to recognize our lack of faith in any given circumstance; but that is all we do, recognize it and deal with it accordingly. This man knew he had unbelief and in his life and in his heart and he asked Christ to help with his doubts. Yes, you can ask God for help with your unbelief, your lack of faith—You can ask God for anything! And He will help you.

"So then faith comes by hearing, and hearing by the word of God" (Romans 10:17).

The Word of God is always our starting point and our ending point for our faith. Our God is limitless, there is nothing, no "thing," impossible for Him. Take this awesome God you serve out of the box of your mind. We are finite creatures in this realm, but when you move into the spiritual realm in Christ we become like Him and we are infinite in His ways! It is time you take this step of faith into the realm of God.

Chapter Fourteen

Faith comes by hearing the word of God. When Jesus was teaching in the synagogue in Jerusalem, He says this in Luke 4:18-21,

> "The Spirit of the Lord is upon Me,
> Because He has anointed Me
> To preach the gospel to the poor;
> He has sent Me to heal the brokenhearted,
> To proclaim liberty to the captives
> And recovery of sight to the blind,
> To set at liberty those who are oppressed;
> To proclaim the acceptable year of the Lord.'
> Then He closed the book, and gave it back to the attendant and sat down. And the eyes of all who were in the synagogue were fixed on Him. And He began to say to them, 'Today this Scripture is fulfilled in your hearing.'"

Today this scripture is fulfilled because you hear this word and see this Word before you! Jesus is the Word of God manifested in the flesh. (See John 1:14.) He spoke the word concerning Himself and told those listening that this word is now before them in His essence. The prophetic word spoken in Isaiah 61 had manifested in the Person of Jesus Christ, the Son of God, and this Word was now before the people. The word was fulfilled because the people heard the spoken word of Christ through The Word—CHRIST! My God, You are amazing in the revelation You give your children.

Your faith will increase as you read and speak the word of God, that is, speak Christ. He is the Word. As you hear Him, your faith will bring you to places you never thought possible. It is time to release not only your faith through the word, but also your faith through the prophetic realm of Jesus Christ. Jesus fulfilled not only this prophecy in Isaiah, but all the prophecies spoken of Him throughout the entire Old Testament and the New Testament, through the ministry of John, the Baptist. He is the spirit of prophecy. He is the essence of the prophetic word spoken.

"And I fell at his feet to worship him. But he said to me, 'See that you do not do that! I am your fellow servant, and of your brethren who have the testimony of Jesus. Worship God! For the testimony of Jesus is the spirit of prophecy'" (Revelation 19:10).

The word "testimony" in the Greek is *martyria* (root for our English word "martyr"), meaning, "to testify, witness or record." While the word "Spirit" is the word *pneuma* which means "breath, blow, air, spirit, and the character of prophecy by which prophets are governed."[23] As we continue we seek revelation; the word "prophecy" which is the Greek word *prophetei*, meaning "divine inspirations declaring the purposes of God; the spirit of prophecy; the divine mind, to which the prophetic faculty is due." The root of this word means, "to bubble up."[24] When you re-write this Scripture with the words that actually describe the word, this is how it reads: "The witness, that is the record, of Jehovah is Salvation is the breath of divine inspirations declaring the purpose of God"

---

23   Strong's Concordance
24   Strong's Concordance

This scripture defines the testimony or witness of Jesus Christ Himself as being the heart of (synonymous with) the Spirit of prophecy. Jesus will be at the center of it all. When we prophesy by faith we speak Jesus! That is what "great faith" is all about! In the two instances of "great faith" mentioned by Christ Himself, the man and the woman of faith went beyond the natural and stepped into the prophetic realm of Christ. Your faith in Christ will bring you to a place inside this prophetic realm of God.

"I have declared the former things from the beginning; They went forth from My mouth, and I caused them to hear it. Suddenly I did them, and they came to pass" (Isaiah 48:3). When Christ speaks, the word He says comes to pass; this kingdom principle is what this man and woman in the scriptures applied in their lives; setting aside every doubt and speaking to dead situations; changing their lives, manifesting those things that were not as though they did exist. (See Romans 4:17.) Their faith was released in the words they spoke, words that went past the natural into the spirit and brought forth what they desired at that time! The things that were theirs in the spirit realm, they spoke out, moving them into this realm.

Prophetic words spoken will pour life into the dead and bring forth God's will, His life, on earth as it is in heaven. You can change your circumstances by standing with God and having faith in Him. Believe and speak the words of Christ; that is, speak Him. Faith and the prophetic are linked in a deeper realm than you may know. Faith in Christ is bringing forth His prophetic vision for your life and for His kingdom.

The centurion and the woman with the demon-possessed daughter both stepped into the prophetic realm of Christ. They saw past today and walked into tomorrow by faith. They did not desire to stay in the same place they were and therefore they did something about it. They moved in and with Christ. They both touched Him with great faith as they peered into the spirit realm of possibilities; they saw what they wanted, and by faith they took what they needed speaking forth the future in Christ.

This book is intended to open the eyes of the Body of Christ—the Church Herself—to walk into the realm of God, receiving what He has already prepared for Her. If you were looking for a book with a 10-point list telling you how to get to the place of great faith, this isn't the book for you. This book was written as a starting point for you to begin to seek God and look deep into the realm where He abides, knowing this is the place He desires for you to be; close with Him in worship, unlocking the hidden things, the invisible things, before your very eyes! The language I speak of is not so much a language as we know it, no, I speak of language as the "venue" of faith. "Venue" is defined as "the place where something happens."

> Now the whole earth had one language and one speech. And it came to pass, as they journeyed from the east, that they found a plain in the land of Shinar, and they dwelt there. Then they said to one another, "Come, let us make bricks and bake them thoroughly." They had brick for stone, and they had asphalt for mortar. And they said, "Come, let us build ourselves a city, and a tower whose top is in the heavens; let us make a name for ourselves, lest we be scattered abroad over the face of the whole earth." But the Lord came down to see the city and the tower which the sons of men had built. And

the Lord said, "Indeed the people are one and they all have one language, and this is what they begin to do; now nothing that they propose to do will be withheld from them. Come, let Us go down and there confuse their language, that they may not understand one another's speech." So the Lord scattered them abroad from there over the face of all the earth, and they ceased building the city. Therefore its name is called Babel, because there the Lord confused the language of all the earth; and from there the Lord scattered them abroad over the face of all the earth.

Genesis 11:1-9

The word "language" is the Hebrew word *saphah* (*sä·fä'*), it is defined as "lip, language, speech, shore, bank, brink, brim, side, edge, border, binding."[25] In this verse this word can mean "tongue or dialect." Something was happening here at the Tower of Babel! The people were all speaking the same thing, unfortunately it was not a righteous thing; nonetheless, they were in one accord in faith and what they wanted to accomplish. Could you imagine if the body of Christ got a hold of this truth what we could accomplish on earth for the glory of God?

Oh, my sweet brother and sister in Christ, how He loves you and wants to see you persevere and press in to Him. Your faith will take you into a deeper relationship with Father, Jesus Christ, and Holy Spirit. God is love. God is about intimacy. His heart is to share with you all He is. Open your eyes to see and your ears to hear what the Spirit of the Lord is saying to

---

25   Strong's Concordance

you today! Now faith is—NOW!

I pray that the Father of all creation spoke to you through His Word, Jesus Christ, and in the power of His Precious Holy Spirit in the pages of this book. Blessings…

Do you know Jesus Christ as your Lord and Savior? If not, know this, He wants to know you. Speak this prayer aloud right where you are:

Heavenly Father, thank You for Your Son Jesus Christ. I believe He came and died for me on the cross and once buried He rose again from the grave and is now sitting at Your right hand. Thank You, Jesus, for dying for my sins. I ask forgiveness for those sins and repent and turn my heart to You.

> "But what does it say? 'The word is near you, in your mouth and in your heart' (that is, the word of faith which we preach): **that if you confess with your mouth the Lord Jesus and believe in your heart that God has raised Him from the dead, you will be saved.** For with the heart one believes unto righteousness, and with the mouth confession is made unto salvation. For the Scripture says, 'Whoever believes on Him will not be put to shame.' For there is no distinction between Jew and Greek, for the same Lord over all is rich to all who call upon Him. For 'whoever calls on the name of the Lord shall be saved.'"
>
> Romans 10:8-13

Maybe you already know Jesus Christ as your Lord and Savior, and yet, you are struggling in some areas in your life. I agree with you that God is here for you and He loves you.

Heavenly Father, there is none like You and I thank You that You alone are God. I believe You love me. I want to seek Your Holy Spirit for guidance, and I believe You have the best for me in Your heart. I search Your ways and release my own will and plans to You. I believe! Help my unbelief! Help me to see Your love and plan for me as I no longer listen to the spirit of fear. I choose to listen to Holy Spirit and Your plan for me—I walk in faith in You! I thank You for all You are and all You have already done for me through Your Son, Jesus Christ! Let me see past myself and into the realm where Your word is established and walk by faith in the heavenly realm with You. Open my eyes to see and my ears to hear what Holy Spirit would reveal to me. Thank You Father for Your heart of love for me.

Prophetess Brenda Eagans abides in Georgetown, Texas, with her husband Windell and together they have a ministry, Radical Fire Ministries. Their heart is to teach the truth of the Word of God, especially regarding the prophetic and the misunderstood prophet. Prophetess Brenda's heart is to raise up prophets in this day and time; prophets of integrity and character in Jesus Christ. She is a mentor and leader of the prophetic realm, bringing forth His will on earth as it is in heaven. If you are interested in contacting Prophetess Brenda Eagans, her information is below:

Brenda Eagans
PO Box 5938
Round Rock, Texas 78683
prophetessoffire@gmail.com

CPSIA information can be obtained
at www.ICGtesting.com
Printed in the USA
BVHW051129010821
613366BV00017B/1355